More Praise for *Embrace the Chaos*

"In this noisy, fast-paced world, it is hard not to get swept away by the demands, anxieties, and challenges that daily come down upon us. *Embrace the Chaos* shows us that only by opening our minds and our hearts to life's wonderful unpredictability can we truly live. It is a wise and welcome book."
—**Marcus Buckingham, author of** *First, Break all the Rules* **and** *Now, Discover Your Strengths*

"Bob has offered an insightful and thought-provoking guide to navigating times of profound change."
—**Ian Read, Chairman and CEO, Pfizer Inc.**

"In a world where change, uncertainty, and continual reinvention have become the new norm, Bob Miglani takes us on a powerful and optimistic journey of quite literally embracing the chaos and organically transforming the future from threat into opportunity and optimism. Read *Embrace the Chaos* and believe it."
—**Henry S. Lodge, coauthor of the** *New York Times* **bestselling** *Younger Next Year* **and** *Younger Next Year for Women*

"Over 2,500 years ago, the Buddha taught his followers about the impermanent nature of existence…explaining how everything is constantly changing, ever flowing, eternally in flux. But our Western minds crave stability, certainty, predictability, and control. 'Give it up,' Bob Miglani tells us in his new book. 'Your longing for control is futile. The truth of reality is chaos. Learn to go with the flow. Relax— and dance with the chaos.' The Buddha would agree. Therein lies freedom and happiness."
—**BJ Gallagher, coauthor of** *Being Buddha at Work*

"If we are going to continue to thrive in these times of profound change, we must learn how to embrace the chaos. This is a most compelling book that offers men and women everywhere hope, inspiration, and courage."
—**Ambassador Paula J. Dobriansky, former Under Secretary of State**

"We all can benefit from Bob's experience in learning to embrace the chaos of our modern life. This book is enormously helpful to me in navigating the everyday challenges of being a husband, father, and NFL official."
—**Carl Johnson, the NFL's first full-time on-field game official**

"Whether we're trying to transform education or change our own lives, it's about embracing chaos. Bob's wonderful book helps show us how to move purposefully and happily through the complex nature of work and life."
—**John Katzman, founder of The Princeton Review, 2U, and Noodle**

"Embrace this book! Bob articulates so perfectly the feelings we all have of uncertainty in life. His fascinating stories and unique observations offer a positive-thinking picture of what we need to get unstuck and move forward successfully."
—**Lynda Bekore, Managing Editor, SmallBizClub.com, and *Huffington Post* blogger**

"'Embrace the chaos' is not just a mantra for management—it's a mantra for life. We can all learn from and enjoy this simple but beautifully written book. It is, without question, worth the read."
—**John J. Connolly, EdD, President and CEO, Castle Connolly Medical Ltd., and former President, New York Medical College**

"With a jolt, Bob's writing forces us to rethink our lives and transform ourselves—to step back from the daily roller coaster of life, savor every passing minute with a free spirit, and discover unlimited potential in ourselves! An easy-to-read manual of life!"
—**Deepak Ahuja, CFO, Tesla Motors**

EMBRACE THE CHAOS

EMBRACE THE
CHAOS

How India Taught Me to Stop
Overthinking and Start Living

BOB MIGLANI

BK

Berrett–Koehler Publishers, Inc.
San Francisco
a BK Life book

Berrett-Koehler Publishers, Inc.
235 Montgomery Street, Suite 650
San Francisco, CA 94104-2916
Tel: (415) 288-0260   Fax: (415) 362-2512   www.bkconnection.com

Ordering Information

Quantity sales. Special discounts are available on quantity purchases by corporations, associations, and others. For details, contact the "Special Sales Department" at the Berrett-Koehler address above.

Individual sales. Berrett-Koehler publications are available through most bookstores. They can also be ordered directly from Berrett-Koehler: Tel: (800) 929-2929; Fax: (802) 864-7626; www.bkconnection.com

Orders for college textbook/course adoption use. Please contact Berrett-Koehler: Tel: (800) 929-2929; Fax: (802) 864-7626.

Orders by U.S. trade bookstores and wholesalers. Please contact Ingram Publisher Services, Tel: (800) 509-4887; Fax: (800) 838-1149; E-mail: customer.service @ingrampublisherservices.com; or visit www.ingrampublisherservices.com/ Ordering for details about electronic ordering.

Berrett-Koehler and the BK logo are registered trademarks of Berrett-Koehler Publishers, Inc.

Printed in the United States of America

Berrett-Koehler books are printed on long-lasting acid-free paper. When it is available, we choose paper that has been manufactured by environmentally responsible processes. These may include using trees grown in sustainable forests, incorporating recycled paper, minimizing chlorine in bleaching, or recycling the energy produced at the paper mill.

Library of Congress Cataloging-in-Publication Data
Miglani, Bob.
Embrace the chaos : how India taught me to stop overthinking and start living / Bob Miglani. — First Edition.
    pages cm
Includes index.
ISBN 978-1-60994-825-2 (pbk.)
1. Self-confidence.   2. Self-control.   3. Resilience (Personality trait)   4. Goal (Psychology) I. Title.
BF575.S39M54 2013
650.1—dc23
                        2013015984

First Edition
19 18 17 16 15 14 13   10 9 8 7 6 5 4 3 2 1

Interior design: Laura Lind Design   *Copy editor:* Elissa Rabellino
Cover design: Kirk DouPonce/DogEared   *Proofreader:* Henrietta Bensussen
          Design   *Indexer:* Erica Caridio
Production: Linda Jupiter Productions

This book is dedicated to all who feel stuck and who overthink about an uncertain future. I believe in the power of our minds and bodies to take positive steps to make a lasting contribution to the work we do, to the people we love, and the lives we lead. I hope the stories in this book serve as a reminder to keep moving forward because our voices, our words, our work, our love, and our actions are needed right here and right now.

CONTENTS

Part 3: Move Forward   73

FOREWORD

Our lives are more chaotic than we'd like. And that's not going to change.

Finding meaning in the busy routines of work and life is never easy. Our daily lives often lack a sense of purpose—a reason to get up in the morning—and appear to serve no apparent end. That can change. This book helps us make that change.

To change, we need to push the Pause button, to see beneath the surface to the place where we know not just with the mind but also with the heart. There are steps we can take to enhance our ability to pause and reflect on our lives.

Bob Miglani offers us simple, practical steps that will help us overcome our hurry sickness—being stressed out, burned out, or just plain stuck.

But first, let's look at the cost of hurry sickness.

When I reflect upon the necessity for introspection in my coaching work, my clients respond, "Who has the time?" or "I'm too busy." That is precisely the problem. Hurry sickness—always going somewhere, never being anywhere—is numbing our conscious awareness of what's really going on in our lives. Our very sense of humanity—our full presence in our own lives—is being hijacked by busyness.

The first step to recovering from hurry sickness is to read this book. It helps us unmask our illusions. It helps us confront those parts of our busyness that are expressions of our real purpose in life. When we lose touch with our purpose, we lose our perspective on what truly matters. And mattering matters, to all of us.

When things are going smoothly, we may not sense the need at all, but when chaos grips our lives, we're forced to reflect. This book awakens us to the reality of the new normal: pause now or pay later.

Bob teaches us that we're never alone on our journey. In order to know people, we must listen to their stories. But we live in an age when we rarely have the time to listen or to hear each other's stories. When we're hurrying, we rarely really know anyone. Instead, we live on the *assumption* that we know each other.

This book is filled with funny, surprising, even moving stories. Bob's own stories of his experiences in India alone are worth the read. And those stories will help you recall your own story and listen to the stories of others.

Bob advises us that remembering the impermanence of life each day helps us to bring greater purpose to our step. He counsels trying to meditate amid the chaos.

Try this: Tomorrow morning, get up a little earlier. Mind over mattress! Before you start your day, sit quietly for five minutes and take three deep breaths. Breath one—just be present. Breath two—be grateful. Breath three—read a paragraph of this book. Picture your day. Picture the possible purpose moments—times when you can serve a cause, a project you care about, or a person you love. You cannot control the chaos. You can control you. One day at a time. One breath at a time.

Embracing the Chaos helps us slow down to the speed of story. It teaches us how to find fulfillment and meaning in a stressed-out world. It teaches us to live with chaos, cope with it, deal with it, accept it, and move forward.

Richard Leider

Author of *Repacking Your Bags, The Power of Purpose,* and *Life Reimagined*

PREFACE

Stress had become my new norm and anxiety was my new best friend. I was stuck in limbo, paralyzed by what I perceived to be an insurmountable problem: a complex, increasingly uncertain, highly unpredictable, interconnected, fast life full of shocks and surprises. The more I thought about trying to plan my future, the more stressed and anxious I became. Each path that lay in front of me looked worse than the other.

Every two weeks, it seemed, my boss (who is actually a good guy) walked into my office and, seated comfortably, asked if I had "found anything yet," because he wasn't sure how long he had before he might have to lay me off. He wasn't being mean; he wasn't sure how long he had himself, and he was trying to be genuinely helpful in the increasingly uncertain world of corporate America.

It's not supposed to be this way, I thought as I walked into my house in the suburbs of New Jersey one evening, after a two-hour commute from the city. Something just doesn't feel right. I mean, I did all that I was supposed to do.

When my family moved to the United States in 1979 with only $75, we embraced the American dream. My parents had two jobs, working seven days a week for years. As I got older, I helped as well as I could by delivering newspapers, mowing lawns, and eventually helping to run our family's Dairy Queen store, which we bought using some family loans and money we saved after coming to America. I put myself through college and got a decent education—even an MBA—by going to school at night. After college, I went to work for a big company, surviving and at times even thriving, for twenty years. I was a number one sales rep, an innovator who started new initiatives and produced solid returns for the company. I worked hard, getting up early and going to bed late. I stuck to my to-do lists, read all the great books, eagerly sought advice from smart mentors, and just kept delivering results as well as I could. I thought I was doing well.

I believed in the idea that if I simply worked hard and smart, I would be successful and happy. I followed all the rules and did all the right things—even got a thirty-year fixed mortgage for a house I knew we could afford. So why did I now feel I was not keeping up? Why was I always worried? A constant chatter of overthinking was keeping me up at night. I felt constantly tense, anxious, and pessimistic about an uncertain future.

It may seem strange, but as I walked into work in New York City each morning, my greatest triumph came from seeing the green light appear on the turnstile as I swiped my corporate ID, signaling that I was still employed. But that little triumph quickly wore off when I got into my office, where I was supposed to be creating, innovating, and driving new opportunities and ideas for our business. How could I move forward when I felt so uncertain about my own job, about the economy, about world events? Even the new ideas I was considering proposing to my boss felt as though they wouldn't pass the huge hurdle that my own overthinking mind threw up against them, leaving me to shrug and stop trying.

I always used to be enthusiastic and positive. How did I start overthinking and, as a result, feeling so worried?

As I lay awake in bed for most of the night, my mind couldn't deal with how to cope with the uncertainty I noticed everywhere I looked: I'm paying more for my two kids' day care than I did for one year of college not too long ago. How am I going to be able to afford $200,000 for each of them when they're ready for college? I know college is years away, but where am I going to get all that money? I'd love to save on the day care and send them to the public school, but like so many local governments in America, my town is broke and doesn't have a full-day kindergarten. How am I supposed to look after my aging parents with both my wife and I working? They don't have a 401(k); they're just a hard-working older couple who run a tiny Dairy Queen ice cream store.

But it wasn't only economics making me feel this way; it was everything. I had lots of friends on Facebook but I somehow felt as though I didn't really know them anymore. I couldn't remember the last time I had gotten together with friends solely for the purpose of shooting the breeze. And although my kids are fairly good at playing Angry Birds on the iPhone, will they be able to have a decent conversation with someone during a job interview? Will they have the hustle and the hunger to compete for jobs against the kids from Shanghai or New Delhi?

Of course, turning on the TV or reading a newspaper didn't help one bit. From the chaos in the Middle East to the debt crises here at home and in Europe, I continued to get more anxious and pessimistic.

Did someone change the formula for life?

Everything I thought was certain was no longer so. There was uncertainty at my job (if I continued to have a job);

stress in trying to balance home, kids, and work; unpredictability in starting a new business with my wife; and the challenge of helping my parents figure out their retirement. I felt overwhelmed, underprepared, and always worried about an increasingly uncertain future.

I was stuck. Paralyzed. Frozen. I stopped making any decisions or choices. At work, I stopped coming up with new ideas and I felt disengaged. Everything was so uncertain and moving so fast that I just didn't know what to do. I thought about moving to another job or another company, but I held back because I thought about all the negatives of an uncertain new career path. I overanalyzed everything and felt in control of nothing. As a result, my career stagnated and I felt like I was slipping down a spiral of anxiety, frustration, and self-doubt.

The root cause of my inability to move forward was that I felt as if my life—at home and at work—no longer had any order to it. I used to know the formula for life and work, but now everything was different. I was trying to identify the new rules in a changing world. I was trying to define the right path to success. But I was having trouble planning for next week; how was I going to plan a five-year career track? I couldn't figure out the direction to take in my life so became stuck. I felt as if I no longer had control over my own destiny.

Then something unexpected happened that changed my life forever. My friend Ben asked me to accompany him on his first business trip to India, and I said yes.

I was born in India and lived there for a part of my youth. More recently, I had been there for family weddings, to visit relatives with my wife, to introduce my kids to their distant cousins, and occasionally for work. I was delighted to take a week of vacation from my job to help Ben figure out how to do business in one of the world's most populous and rapidly growing economies.

Ben's face became more perplexed as the week wore on and he experienced all that is India—cows on the road; confusing business meetings; the way people pray, shop, or stand in line (what line?); the way life keeps moving, fast.

As we prepared to leave India and we reflected on his busy week of meeting people and trying to understand the culture, Ben asked, in an exhausted voice, "How does anything get done in a country that is filled with so much craziness and confusion—on the roads, in meetings, in daily life—whether it's going to the market to buy food, competing against so many others to find a job, getting a postage stamp at the post office, or trying to do a business deal? There is so much chaos here. How does it work with a billion people? I just don't get it. How do people figure out what to do when they have no idea what's going to happen next?"

I answered, "Well, that's India for you. It's a chaotic place. But let me ask you this: Have you ever been to an Indian wedding in the U.S.?"

"No," he said. "Why do you ask?"

"Because an Indian wedding will teach you how to deal with uncertainty," I answered. "Here's what I mean. You go to an Indian wedding and you experience an all-out attack on all your senses. There's confusion everywhere. People are running late; you don't know what's going on. So many colors, smells, music, dancing, and new outfits you've never seen before. Some people arguing, others laughing, some drinking, some praying. Marigold flowers everywhere—in a vase and all over the floor!

"There's a horse or an elephant (yes, even at Indian weddings in the U.S.), and you're not quite sure, but it's not for the kids. Nothing ever goes according to plan or according to what is written on the invitation. You feel like you have no control and no idea what's going to happen next. Instead of a celebration, it feels more like a riot. It's total chaos. But five or eight hours later, two people get married! They do get married!

"What you have to remember is that, while you may not be able to know what happens next and you feel as though there's no order to anything, two people *will* get married, and everything will seem perfect when it's all over. It all works out in the end. Just accept it. You just have to let go and go with the flow that leads you up to the end. Enjoy the ride! If you focus too much on trying to figure out or control what comes next, you'll miss the best time of your life and it will all be over before you know it.

"You have to change your mind-set and embrace the chaos," I exclaimed.

And so *Embrace the Chaos* was born!

As I returned home to the suburbs of New Jersey, to my own life and career uncertainty, I reflected on my talk with Ben. And suddenly I realized that what I was trying to tell my friend to do in India was exactly what I needed to do to help reduce my stress and move forward in my own life, in my own career, right here at home in America. I was spending too much time worrying about the noise of the wedding rather than enjoying the spectacle.

To be honest, I didn't feel as frustrated or anxious in India, even though things are so much harder there. India is a country of more than 1.2 billion people living in a country about one-third the size of the United States. Add to this the complexity of many languages and customs as well as a highly fragmented and complex economy with lots of chaos. Frankly, the place just shouldn't work at all. Yet, according to one international rating (the Happy Planet Index), India far outstrips the United States in happiness. What was the secret sauce they had that I didn't?

In order to learn how to embrace the chaos of my life in the United States, I realized, I would have to reclaim my past. I would learn how to move forward in chaos from the most chaotic place I knew: India.

YOU HAVE LESS CONTROL THAN YOU THINK. GET OVER IT!

At the heart of so much of our stress and anxiety about feeling stuck in uncertainty lies a feeling that we have no control. Whether we are thinking about our jobs, our kids, our relationships, our colleagues and the people around us, the economy, or our politics, we have a deep desire to have some level of control over our lives. We *need* to be in control. We worry and get caught up in overthinking and overanalyzing what lies ahead because we so badly want our future to turn out the way we want, within our realm of control.

Somewhere along our journey in life, however, things don't work out as we expect them to, no matter how hard we try to control things. This is especially true in our new global, hyperconnected, superfast world, where things are so complicated and random events and changes occur seemingly out of nowhere. As a result, we get overwhelmed and consumed by the chaos, unable to move forward.

We attempt to control but we cannot. We may control the neighborhood where we choose to live but we can't control our neighbors. We may choose the place where we work but we can't control our bosses, colleagues, or customers. We have some control over the seat we want on the plane but we can't control who's seated next to us or whether the flight will be late. We choose our friends but we cannot control what they say or think. We can barely control our own children, so how can we possibly control the essence of life itself?

We think we have control but we don't. And this scares us. This loss of control is the root of much of our stress and overthinking.

In the beginning, it was difficult for me to accept that we may never have had control over life in the first place, because it's contrary to everything I was taught while growing up. We plan our education, map out our career, decide on our relationships, and make important life decisions or choices based on this very notion that we have some kind of order, some control, a plan.

For a long time I fought this idea of letting go of control—as any reasonable person would when trying to let go of something that is so attached to the very fiber of his or her being. But the stress and overthinking was hurting me from the inside out. Luckily, through some unexpected, fun, and interesting experiences in the country, which destroyed any notions of order and control, I was forced to let go, and I realized that we can never really conquer the chaos. We can only embrace it.

And after we embrace it, we can start reveling in it.

Letting go of control is a wonderfully freeing experience that opens us up to new, fresh possibilities. It leads us down paths we never would have walked, introducing us to new people, new opportunities, and some of the best experiences in our lives. It brings out strengths we never knew existed inside of us. It brings forward ideas hidden inside, which helps us to create, develop, and flourish. It allows us to live freely because we're no longer feeling as though we're carrying the burden of the world on our shoulders.

"Do you want me to just give up and wait for things to happen?" you might ask.

Not exactly. What I'm suggesting is not that we sit back and give up on life but that we in fact work harder on the things that we can control: our own words, thoughts, and actions. By making a choice to redirect our frequently wasted effort to control others or the conditions around us, by refocusing that intense passion on our own actions, living in each precious moment, we can begin to move forward into a life we want. This is really the only certainty we have: ourselves.

It isn't easy to redirect that control to ourselves, but there are three principles I developed while learning to embrace the chaos in a confusing place like India. I've organized the main parts of this book around these three principles.

First, accept. By accepting the unpredictable, uncertain, imperfect, and complicated nature of life, we can begin to let go of the past, let go of plans gone wrong, let go of our narrative of the way life ought to be and begin focusing on the way it is. We must accept that the only control we have is over ourselves.

Second, don't overthink. Let's stop overanalyzing, overplanning, or trying to predict what will happen tomorrow. We spend so much time thinking about the future, which we cannot control anyway, that we miss some of the best times of our lives, happening around us right now.

Third, move forward. Take action. Taking charge of ourselves, our goals, our purpose, our thoughts, our words, our actions, and the way we navigate the chaos—these are the things are that are completely within our control. When we are armed with knowledge of our own resilience, taking action can create more certainty than waiting around for perfection.

o   o   o

This book covers a series of trips I took to India over the past twenty years that helped me rediscover the joy of living by letting go of my illusions of control, order, and perfection. I realize that telling stressed-out readers to let go and stop trying to control everything is about as helpful as telling someone in a rainstorm to not get wet. So my approach in this book is less to share advice and principles—although I can't help doing that from time to time—than to invite you to join me on these trips and see these Embrace the Chaos moments in action.

Even the details of the trips are secondary to the people, the ordinary Indians, described in these chapters. In this remarkable country of confusion, chaos, and celebration, more than a billion people are trying, working, loving, exploring, living, and moving forward, often with a quiet joy that cannot be stopped. They are my teachers and my inspiration, and not a day goes by when I don't use something that I learned from them.

I don't expect many readers will ever travel to India, but I find stories from India can be useful in anyone's daily life because India is a country bursting with what I believe to be the four forces of chaos that cause so many of us stress and worry: uncertainty, unpredictability, complexity, and speed. Go on a journey anywhere—to a tourist destination or to a business meeting—and things have a way of going wrong. You get lost, find yourself stuck in the middle of complicated situations, and always run into some sort of roadblock. There are rituals being performed in numerous places of worship; constant power outages; dilapidated infrastructure; and frequent political infighting, strikes, and rallies, from the villages to the modern steel metropolises.

The inequalities also are stark. A child no older than three, wearing a torn, dirty, oversized shirt and no underpants, sits by the side of the road, barely paying attention to the horns of the little white cars buzzing by. Meanwhile, a stone's throw away, the Burberry boutique beckons New Delhi's elite.

In addition, Indians face the complexity of dozens of languages, endless regulations, and the unpredictability of companies being shut down or shifting business models.

In India, one doesn't know what's going to happen next or when it's going to happen, and when it does happen, it seems scary and comes out of nowhere, fast! The place has a way of completely destroying any notions of control that we think we have. As a visitor, you get frustrated, exhausted, sick in the stomach (not always from the food), overwhelmed, anxious, stressed, and plain old angry, finding yourself with no control over anything. You don't know what's going to happen next and you don't know which way to go.

It's when things seem the most hopeless and tense, however, that you find yourself letting go and going with the flow. Something happens out of nowhere and things change, and suddenly you realize that it's starting to turn around.

Somehow, through a great deal of churning, things work out in the end—not as you expected, but sometimes even better.

And you realize it wasn't so bad after all. In fact, you're a transformed person, finding joy and fulfillment in the smallest things. Liberated from the shackles of an orderly framework that your mind no longer needs to control, you begin to stop analyzing life and start living it.

India is a place of extremes, contradictions, and inequities, but there's something about it that wakes you up to the realities of life. For me, India's allure was not in the perspective it provided me, the understanding that they have so little while we have so much more back home and I ought to be grateful for that. It wasn't about "Eat your broccoli, kid, because kids in India are starving." Instead, the allure of India as a training ground was that, despite crumbling infrastructure, a complex society of many different castes, cultures, and languages, and extreme poverty and awful conditions, people continue to be happy. They forge ahead in their lives and their work, sometimes with joy in their eyes, kindness in their hearts, and passionate effort. Despite the unpredictability, Indians continue to move forward.

As I looked back over twenty years of experience in India, I started to learn and grow. Observations led to insight. Insight led me to a better understanding of how people in India move forward in life and work without having grandiose plans, expectations, or forecasts.

Once I began to notice the invisible fabric that helps tie Indians together in their day-to-day lives, I began to feel less stressed and anxious about my own life. I started to catch myself overanalyzing and overthinking, and I began reminding myself to let go of my past notions and to keep moving forward.

After reflecting on what I had learned and putting these valuable lessons into practice, I became less worried about the future and started to become more engaged in life. At work, I began creating again, developing new ideas and solutions and, with the support of my boss, implementing those ideas to good effect. At home, I became more relaxed, reveling in the daily adventures with the kids, in helping them with their homework, in teaching them to play sports, and taking advantage of every moment. I also started trying new things and explored writing again, sharing my thoughts and learning to help others as well as I could. Little by little, my writing gained momentum, eventually leading me to write this book.

Although the uncertainties and unpredictable nature of life didn't go away, I learned to cope with it better. Ultimately, I realized that learning to embrace the chaos was not about fixing my career or quitting my job to live on some faraway island devoid of any chaos (although that does sound appealing). For me, it is more about learning to take action and to participate in life, accepting that the chaos of modern life will continue to exist—with or without my approval—and choosing to move forward anyway.

PART 1

Accept

Accept and let go of trying to control the chaos out there. Let's control the chaos in our own minds and the actions we take each day.

Accept that life is uncertain, unpredictable, complicated, and fast. Accept the impermanence and imperfections. Accept both the ups and the downs. By learning to stop trying to bring our narrative of order and perfection to life, which actually has no order, we can start the process of living again.

Accept that there is no perfect job, no perfect person, no perfect relationship, and no perfect life. There are only jobs, people, relationships, and life. Accept it all as it is—good, bad, great, short, up-and-down, awful, crazy, and every way in between.

Life has always been chaotic, and it gets more complicated as the world progresses forward with ever more people. Let's get used to it.

Accept that we cannot control life. We can only control ourselves—our thoughts, our words, and our actions.

Accept that we have always had a choice to think differently, to take action, to move forward, to use our own hands, to create, to innovate, to do, to live.

Let go of all the old baggage. Let go of the ego. Let go of the way things used to be or the way you think they ought to be.

Let go of past relationships, past ways of working, and the need to hang on to something that isn't there anymore. Let go of trying to bring your order and your expectations to the outside world.

Stop trying to control what crosses your path. Just control yourself.

I know this kind of acceptance is a tall order—few can practice it consistently or perfectly. For some, it may take a lifetime to master. Many will even criticize this kind of acceptance as passiveness, weakness, or defeatism. Shouldn't we always pull out the stops to fight something that's bothering us?

However, the practice of acceptance is a "don't knock it until you try it" kind of principle, as the following stories will attempt to show.

CHAPTER 1

DRIVING ON INDIAN
ROADS

You cannot control the chaos.
You can control you.

Every day we hear about and see uncertainty in everything. We think about all the things we could be doing differently in our lives but we hold back because there are so many paths in front of us and they have no predictable and appealing outcomes. We consider going in one direction but then our minds start overanalyzing and overthinking all the possible problems we may encounter. "Yes, but . . ." starts coming out of our mouths almost immediately, restraining our hearts, which want to go forward. Our minds accentuate the negatives without any effort. We get so overwhelmed with all the chaos that lies in front of us that we find ourselves standing still, unable to move forward.

In a word, everything seems to be out of control.

But is that such a bad thing? We can't control other people or how they think or what they'll do. We can't predict what's going to happen with the economy or our jobs. Why create stress for ourselves by worrying about something that might or might not happen? Stop trying to control it. This incessant need to be in control is just a way to stand in the middle of the road while life passes us by.

In a very real sense, this book began during a taxi ride on an Indian road, where I realized how little control we have—and how little that should concern us. Participating in life, despite the chaos that lies ahead in all paths, is our choice and ours alone, and it can be as simple as driving forward in any direction, whatever may come. Because eventually, despite a cow or two blocking the road (as is commonplace throughout India), we will get there just fine.

o o o

During my friend Ben's first visit to India, he joined a small delegation of U.S. businesspeople who were interested in learning about the country and doing business there. An entrepreneur at heart, Ben was excited to learn about how this booming emerging economy of a billion people worked. Because I'm the only Indian American guy he knows, and because I also serve on the board of the United States–India trade group that was taking him on this trip, Ben asked me to join him as his quasilocal guide for a few days. He wanted a friend to guide him so that he wouldn't look like a typical foreigner.

I could sense his trepidation as he and a couple of others gathered around our car, ready to confront a road full of chaos that lay ahead of us in Ahmedabad, a city of roughly six million people. Navigating the city's roads with a local driver was Ben's first experience with uncertainty and shock since he had landed in India. There were no markings on the street and not many traffic lights—and no one paid any attention to the traffic signals anyway. The road was brimming with bicycles, carefree pedestrians, motorcycles, scooters, small trucks, rickshaws, three-wheelers (scooters that serve as small taxicabs), and the occasional cow or buffalo. These were our road companions as our driver weaved through the mess to our destination.

I was worried about making the meetings on time and was anxious because I wasn't sure who was going to show up. I didn't want our trade group to look bad and I felt like I had a lot riding on my shoulders. After all, this was "my" country, which I was trying to show off to Ben and others.

Just then, our car encountered a cow that wouldn't move out of the way, so our driver backed up on a one-way street and found another road. Because, well, that's what you do in India. Relieved that we were progressing toward our destination, I looked back to see the puzzled and amusing reaction of the passengers in the backseat.

The driver was a local, and although he wasn't too knowledgeable about all the roads, he sure knew how to handle moving the car in and out of traffic. I was in front, next to the taxi driver, who sits on the right, and at one point I noticed in the side mirror a motorcycle approaching fast, trying to pass us on our left. Up ahead, also on the left, was a huge tree, and because the Indian custom is to not tear down sacred trees and/or any possible signs of God and so on, the road just sort of went around the right side of the tree.

Our driver started speeding up. This meant that the motorcycle behind and to the left of us was surely going to head right into the tree.

Now, I have built up some immunity over the years of travel in India, but seeing this motorcycle trying to speed up to pass on our left scared me. I thought surely the motorcycle guy was doomed.

I held on tight as we approached the tree. Our car veered slightly to the right and we passed the tree with no problem. I quickly looked behind, expecting the motorcycle to have crashed into the tree. Nothing doing. The motorcycle had simply slowed down and also passed the tree on the right— right behind us.

I looked back at the audience in the rear seat. They had been white before, but they were even whiter now, having lost some color in their faces.

Relieved and somewhat impressed with my new best friend—the driver—I asked in my broken Hindi, "Wasn't that a little close?"

"Not really. What do you mean, sir?" he answered.

I was surprised. "I mean, come on. Didn't you think that guy was going to hit the tree? Weren't you concerned that by speeding up you were risking his chance of getting hurt?"

His answer resonated and has stayed with me. He said, "Sir, in this crazy road, which is my daily life, I have learned that I cannot count on anyone else or anything else to be predictable. Because each road has a surprise. Either a cow comes out of nowhere, another car races to pass, a child's ball enters the road, a scooter or a rickshaw comes out of nowhere, with a total surprise. The only thing I can do is be prepared and think of only my car and the passengers in my car. So the person driving next to me has to take precaution as he needs to, and I should do the same for myself and my passengers only. I can only control my own driving."

Being a passenger in that car made me realize that he was absolutely right. We don't control what we encounter on the road. We only control how we steer our way forward.

CHAPTER 2

SEARCHING FOR GOD
AT FIVE THOUSAND FEET

Let go of plans gone wrong. Things have a
way of working out in the end.

No matter how hard we try to control our plans, things can go wrong. As a result, we may find ourselves in a state of confusion, worrying about everything. We look around for something to blame, and sometimes we blame ourselves for not planning better, as if we have perfect foresight. Other times we focus on the imperfections of everything around us. We blame the chaos itself, feeling as though we are the only one it touches. We may wonder, Why me?

This tension ultimately gives way to anxiety, crippling any action, which we feel would be futile. We find seemingly endless logical reasons not to try anything because, in that mind-set, it feels like it will all end so badly. "What's the point?" we ask, giving up all hope.

But life has a way of constantly shuffling things around, shaking our understanding of what's possible and what's not. And somehow, in some cosmically unpredictable way, life unfolds and things work out—never as expected, but sometimes even better.

o o o

Many years ago, when I was about to graduate college, my parents took my sisters and me to visit Vaishno Devi, a mountaintop holy site where the god Mata Rani is known to reside. Eight million Hindu pilgrims visit the deity each year, walking about 7.5 miles from the main city of Katra, in the state of Jammu and Kashmir, and climbing to an altitude of 5,300 feet.

My two sisters and I were not too keen on going on this journey, but we felt obligated because we had made a commitment to support our mom in her strong religious beliefs. In Hindu culture, it is said that if the thought of going to visit Mata on this mountaintop comes into your head just once, then you must do it to ease the mind. And my mom's mind was zoned in on making the journey. Plus, we wanted to see what the fuss was all about. Was God really up there on this mountain? What really is up there? Deep inside all of us was a hidden spiritual curiosity, and we couldn't give up this chance to satisfy it.

Being the type A person that I am, I took charge of all the preparations—and boy, was I prepared. I had booked the flight from New Delhi into Jammu's only airport. Ascertained the temperature to ensure we all had proper clothing. Figured out how many mountain guides we were going to hire and the prevailing wages so that I could negotiate properly. The backpack was all set with extra scarves, extra socks in case ours got wet, a towel, and a Swiss Army knife—in case, as my sisters joked, we were stranded up there and I had to go hunt for food.

As we were about to leave for the airport in New Delhi, my aunt mentioned that we shouldn't take any belts or wallets made of leather because, being made of animal hide, they wouldn't be allowed inside the holy site. As we rushed out the door, we dropped our wallets and purses with my aunt.

When we got to the airport to check in, it seemed as if every other person cut in front of me at the counter.

"How come there are no lines?" I screamed in frustration at the clerk. "How come there's no order in this place?"

"Sir, please give me your ticket now and I'll check you in," the clerk said, without apologizing for taking the four people who had cut right in front of me.

Landing at Jammu's airport, in the mountains of Kashmir, was truly breathtaking. From the perspective of the metropolitan cities, you tend to forget the true beauty of India. After negotiating with a local taxi driver to take us to the base of the mountain to begin our trek, we felt great—confident, enthusiastic, and happy to begin the journey, prepared to meet God herself.

The narrow, slightly paved path up the mountain was filled with other worshippers, some making the journey up and others on their way down. Many were barefoot. My mom was ahead of the pack and, along with other worshippers, started chanting, "Jai Mata di," which means "in praise of Mata." This chant is often used to bring forth *shakti*, a force or spirit by which one can better shape one's destiny.

The chanting was a little odd to my sisters and me in the beginning, but we started getting into it as the hours passed and we needed some encouragement to keep us moving up the mountain. My dad was not as comfortable. His bad knee prevented him from walking up with us and, as a lot of older worshippers do, he was taking a horse up the mountain, led by the horse's owner.

We made it up the mountain in eight hours, stopping for a bit here and there to go to the bathroom and to drink tea purchased from some of the many makeshift tea, food, and souvenir stands that dotted the mountain path.

It was about 2 a.m. when we arrived at our destination. We stood in front of a tiny passageway carved through the mountain by eons of fresh mountain water from the melting snow. Cold, tired, and a bit hungry, we made our way to the point where we were supposed to deposit all shoes and baggage. After ensuring that we were carrying no leather or other animal materials, the pandits (holy men) showed us toward the washing area, where we used the freezing mountain water to wash our hands, faces, and feet. The idea is to purify yourself before visiting Mata. This is as close to God as you're going to get and you can't be dirty.

My mom rushed to the front of the line, an eager, sincere devotee of Mata. I could sense the humility in her slow, precise washing with the freezing water.

"There's a line here but not in the airports," I remarked snidely.

"I didn't know we were supposed to be going through this tiny little space in a cave," my scared younger sister said to me. She was fearful of small spaces and terrified of going through a cave, worried that it might collapse on her. "I'm not going in there."

My mom went first, followed by my middle sister and then me, holding my younger sister's hand. My dad went last. It was a vertical crevice, only fit for slim people, with little light except for the moonlight on the other side of the cave. Freezing mountain water running down one side was a constant reminder that we were actually inside a real mountain.

I shifted my shoulders toward the side of the cave that had been smoothed by years of running water. Barefoot, I made my way through the cave toward what appeared to be an opening. I could see candles in front of a small shrine representing the semi-exact point where God herself resides. I say "semi-exact" because nothing is ever exact in India.

In an area large enough to hold only two or three people, including the pandits, I stopped and prayed. I looked around to find something that gave some indication of a supernatural force. I'm more spiritual than religious, but I wanted so much to believe. I was genuinely trying to pray, hard, to feel the divine presence. What did I have to lose? Even so, it was dark and I couldn't really make out anything remarkable. All I could think of was how cold the water was beneath my feet.

"Keep moving," said one of the pandits as I started to get into deep thoughts about the existence of God.

Like my sister, I'm not a fan of closed spaces, so I was relieved to get out of the cave. I gave a little smile to my mom, who seemed to be experiencing her own moment of bliss as she took in the *darshan* (visit of God). She was in heaven.

After gathering our belongings, we took in the dark mountain scenery as well as we could at 3 a.m. and then began our journey down the mountain. With sore muscles, hurting backs, and empty bellies, my sisters and I were a little cranky. I gathered everyone around and suggested that we join my dad in taking horses the rest of the way down the mountain. In order to make our flight back to New Delhi and then our flight to the United States the next day, we would need to hurry, and walking wasn't going to cut it.

My sisters leaped at the suggestion but my mom wouldn't have any of it. She preferred to sacrifice in the name of God and to finish the way she had started, on foot. Something about suffering as a way to reach God.

I took charge and negotiated with a couple of horse guys, and the rest of us went galloping down the mountain. OK, it was more like a slow pony ride.

When we reached the base of the mountain, we felt exhausted and really sleepy. "We can all have a nice rest on the plane back to Delhi," I said as I rushed us into the taxi for the airport, trying to keep us all on schedule.

As I gave the woman at the check-in counter our U.S. passports and tickets back to New Delhi, she said casually, "The flight is not operating today, sir."

"I'm sorry. I didn't catch that."

"No flights to Delhi today."

"Sorry, I don't understand. Today is Tuesday and it says here on our ticket that there is a flight to Delhi today."

"Fog today."

"So, you mean it's canceled?"

"No flight today, sir. Fog. Maybe later. Maybe tomorrow."

"I don't understand. Is the flight canceled or is it not?" I asked in a loud and definitive way, signaling the need for certainty on the subject.

I wasn't going to get any certainty. Only later did I learn that, for most Indians, there is no certainty. They'll never tell you a flight is canceled. They'll say that it's not operating today—I guess because "canceled" is very definitive and nothing in India is ever definitive.

Angry, hungry, exhausted, and utterly confused at the lack of any civility, I threw up my hands and walked away, joining my family standing nearby. They had already learned that our flight was "not operating today."

"How are we going to get back to Delhi in time to make our flight home to New York?" My sister asked the obvious question and everyone else turned to me, looking for an answer.

I had no idea. No one else did either.

Being stranded in a small town with an outdated airport, waiting for a flight to resume the next day, is normally no big deal. What made it difficult this time was the hunger, the two days' lack of sleep, the freezing weather, the blisters on my feet from going up and down a mountain, and simply not knowing when we would be going home. The lack of certainty was causing me a great deal of stress and anxiety.

After an hour or so of trying to understand the flight situation as explained by a helpful agent, my mom and dad came back and told us that we would have to wait at the airport until the fog cleared up in Delhi, because they might reopen the flight today. For the time being, the flight was not operating, but it might, eventually. There was still no certainty; it was a maybe. I hated maybes.

"Why can't anyone in this country say something definitively?" I blurted out in frustration.

I couldn't deal with a maybe. I suggested that we take a taxi into town and get something to eat. At least with some food in our stomachs we might be able to think straight.

As we were about to get out of the taxi after a fifteen-minute ride into town, I reached for my wallet. But there was nothing in the back pocket of my jeans.

I felt this "Oh, no" approach all of us in unison. We had left all our wallets and purses back in New Delhi, at my aunt's place, after she reminded us that they don't like leather up at the holy site.

No one had brought a wallet. Each of us had thought someone else was going to, so no one had any money! Zip. Zero. Nada. No rupees. No dollars. Nothing. Whatever loose change we had started out with had been spent on tea on our way up the mountain.

It took me a nanosecond before I began to freak out.

"You have to be kidding me!" I exclaimed.

We were all exhausted and hungry and we had nowhere to stay. No food. No cell phones. And no certainty about our trip back home. All my perfectly laid plans were going out the window. I was freaking out, spinning into a spiral of anxiety.

With the aroma of hot, fried vegetables circling all around us, I stood in the middle of a crowded market, paralyzed. After apologizing to the taxi driver, we found a couple of empty spaces on the cold, exposed brick steps of a restaurant and just sat.

My sisters and I were miserable, thinking and thinking about what to do next, but I couldn't see any way forward. Nothing seemed to bother my dad, though. He sandwiched himself between two local men who were smoking a hookah on a small cot made of rope. At ease with the whole situation, he blended in, almost reveling in the chaos that we were experiencing.

Seeing him so relaxed made me more tense and anxious. How can he relax at a time like this? He's not coming up with any solutions, for crying out loud!

I could taste those savory *pakoras* (fried vegetables) being prepared at the stall next to us. Anxiety started seeping into my mind, like oil from the *pakoras*, dripping into my body. I was debilitated by my stiff neck and arched back, and I felt there was no reasonable path in front of me.

Stressed, worried, and anxious, I sat there, still trying desperately to hold on to the plan that I had not foreseen going wrong. I blamed the airlines and the ticket agent and this crazy country, and I remained so focused on the past plan and what had gone wrong that I became closed to any new ideas.

But my mom was still standing, and she said, "All right, let's go and try to do something at the airport."

"What's the point, Mom?" we all asked.

"We're stuck," I said. "There's no way out of this crummy place. We'll have to suck it up and wait at the stupid airport until tomorrow." Clearly, this confusing country was the cause of our disrupted plans.

She grabbed us by our hands and, pulling us up, calmly said, "Let it go. Just let it go. It happens. Stop trying to figure out why. Let go. Now, come on. Let's go and see if the airline can do something for us. Let's try."

Not wanting to disappoint our mom, we reluctantly got up. We begged a taxi driver to take us back to the airport, promising him money after we secured a solution. He felt sorry for us and gave us a lift to the airport.

"Sorry. No flight today. You can talk to the airline office nearby the airport if you want," the ticket agent responded, after we pleaded with her to find a way to get us back to Delhi in time for our homeward flight.

"See, I told you. There's no point, Mom."

"Keep moving. Let's try the main office. We have nothing to lose," she said.

Thanks to the continued kindness of the taxi driver, we managed to get to the airline's main office, five minutes from the airport.

Feeling as though we were making some progress, and hopeful of finding a solution, we headed into the office. A young man in the customer service department sat us down and essentially gave us the same answer.

"Sorry, flight is canceled today and, weather willing, will fly to Delhi tomorrow. We can't do anything for you. You will have to wait at the airport."

"Is there any other way of getting back to Delhi?" I asked.

"Well, there's the train. You can check to see if the train will reach in time."

This seemed to be all he was going to give us, so I started to say thanks and walk away. But not my mom. She forged ahead, asking very specifically, "Sir, can you please call someone to ask if there is a train going to Delhi today? We are desperate to return and could really use your help."

The young man looked at us and made a call.

"The Rajdhani Express overnight sleeper train is leaving in two hours and there are probably some seats available. You can buy the tickets when you get to the station and it should put you in Delhi in the late morning. You should be able to make your flight back to the U.S. with no problem."

This was a start. But my mom persisted.

"We have no money to buy tickets for the train," she said. "Could you kindly find a way to refund us the money from the flights so that we can buy the train tickets?"

"I'm sorry, but I cannot do that until your flight is officially canceled. Right now, the status is officially delayed, due to fog in Delhi."

"Please. See if you can do something. Please, sir. We need to get home," my mom insisted. She pressed on with sincerity, persuasive enough to warrant the man having a conversation with his manager.

After speaking to his manager, the young man came back and brought us something we never thought we'd see: money! He gave us a refund and said with a smile, "Good luck."

With the money, we would be able to secure a sleeper car and arrive back in Delhi in twelve hours! We ate a little, paid the taxi driver, and headed to the train station. We were able to secure seats on the train to Delhi and even had a few rupees to spare. Plus, we were told that we had first-class tickets and could have access to the station lounge.

Unfortunately, it was more like a Turkish prison than a first-class lounge. I've seen *Midnight Express*!

Sitting on our backpacks, my sisters and I were miserable. But then we noticed our dad, again sitting between two locals. He seemed comfortable, like he belonged there. He had seen this movie before, too, and he was laughing at the punch line that was coming.

That punch line turned out to be the biggest rat I'd ever seen, coming toward us as if to indicate his right-of-way, unafraid of anyone. He was on his own turf, free to roam for food just like the rest of us on the platform, in broad daylight.

My sisters and I burst out laughing—at our exhaustion, at the whole experience of this miserably unorganized, unpredictable country. Lack of proper infrastructure. No one tells you the straight facts. Something always goes wrong.

But it was one of the most memorable and fun moments of my life.

Once on the train, we got into our sleeper compartments, which were decent, though my bed felt like a small wooden door laid flat and suspended by a rope tied to a nail or two.

First class? I thought. Whatever. It really doesn't matter, as long as it takes me home.

It's funny how the imperfections don't bother you so much as long as you feel like you're headed in the right direction.

Then a man came through the cabins, handing out the most savory bit of sustenance I've ever had in my life: two perfectly round *aloo parathas*, Indian bread with potatoes inside. Heavenly. It might have been the greatest meal of my life.

My sisters and I talked, joked, and reveled in the scene outside the window of the Rajdhani Express as it took us back to civilization. My mom was enjoying delicious hot tea with a generous helping of sugar. The air was cool and crisp and we didn't mind the blend of perspiration that floated about the compartment. We were headed home.

We were giddy on that train back to Delhi. We drank tea with a handful of local travelers who told us fascinating stories. Looking out the tiny windows of the Rajdhani Express, we were able to see India in a different way than we saw it while flying through the clouds above.

Feeling the steel of the rails underneath, I started to realize that what I was searching for on the top of that mountain actually already resides deep inside all of us. It is this force, an innate strength that has guided us through history. It is an unshakeable urge to give the body motion, an ability to keep walking, to keep trying, and to continue moving forward despite not knowing what will happen.

What I had missed seeing and feeling five thousand feet above, in my search for the presence of God, I discovered only when I was forced to let go of the plans I had made, when I stopped trying to understand why things went wrong and simply accepted it. Instead, I found that presence hidden inside the generosity and kindness of those who notice our effort and help us on our journey, in the luck and randomness of things all around, and in the encouraging, action-oriented spirit that propelled my mom to let go of overthinking, to accept, to have faith, to believe, and to just keep moving forward.

Looking out the window, smiling at what I had learned, I drifted slowly off to sleep, passing by farmers in fields; huts made of dung, lit inside by kerosene lamps; men on carts pulled by buffalo; and the rolling of a black bicycle rim propelled forward on a dirt road by a stick in motion, carried by the sheer joy of a young boy trying to get home.

CHAPTER 3

TWO GUYS
HOLDING HANDS

You are never alone.

S ometimes we feel as though we are the only ones going through life's problems and challenges. Sitting in the isolated world of a desk, a computer, and a cell phone, among thousands of friends in the virtual world, we sometimes live, shop, drive, and work without speaking to a single human soul. We eat lunch in front of the computer at our desk. We purchase products online without talking to anyone. The birthday phone call has been replaced by a post on our Facebook timeline. We hold conference calls with colleagues in the office next door. An automatic e-mail is sent to a colleague celebrating twenty years of service in the same company, with no phone call or in-person visit with cupcakes.

All of this may leave us feeling isolated and lonely in the real world. Forget the gold watch; sometimes it's just nice to see a human face instead of an e-mail.

Some studies suggest that younger people choose texting over phone conversations because they fear the loss of control a phone call represents. (Who hasn't been stuck on the phone with someone who won't stop talking?) I've seen for myself that colleagues under age thirty will do almost anything to avoid talking on the phone at work.

We have created walls around us that prevent us from bonding with others, even while we create online virtual timelines of our lives for the world to see. But we're so lonely. We're terrified of the uncertainty around and in front of us. Isolated in a hyperconnected virtual world, we lack the most important benefit of society: face-to-face social connections that help keep us going.

A big part of acceptance is accepting other people as they are. This is the joy of social connections: if we stop trying to fix one another, control one another, or judge one another, we can begin to lift each other up. We just have to accept the person we get, not the person we want.

India is full of people who can't escape into a fortress of solitude, even if they tried. From neighbors who stop by unannounced to the social gatherings for every odd occasion, Indians live in a culture of self-imposed socialization. Such social habits, demonstrated on so many levels, can help us face life's challenges, to feel less alone in this crazy world.

It's not perfect or ideal, but those human connections and deep relationships keep Indians going forward, despite living in an unpredictable environment where nothing is certain. The tribal fires around which comforting words of wisdom were dispensed by village elders years ago have become the societal norms of neighbors popping in from time to time, friends meeting friends at tiny celebrations, parents' dinner-table advice to the adult sons and daughters who live with them, and sometimes even through the simple gesture of two guys holding hands, which I had the almost awkward pleasure of experiencing.

o   o   o

While I was on our family trip to the holy mountain, I went to meet one of my many distant cousins, who I hadn't seen for fifteen years. We had spent a lot of years together when we were kids, and because he was a little older than me, he found our reunion particularly special. Remembering our younger times together, he was extremely happy to see me and to meet my family.

As his wife prepared lunch, he suggested we go for a walk in the old neighborhood, to see what had changed and who was still around.

We took his motorcycle around and stopped near a tiny snack shop. After helping me off the motorcycle, he grabbed my hand and just held it. He held my hand while we crossed the busy street, showing me some of the people who were still around, pointing with his other hand to this, that, and the other. But I couldn't concentrate because I was freaking out inside. Why was this guy holding my hand, especially in public? What was the deal?

Feeling very uncomfortable, I tried to free my hand in a way that wouldn't hurt his feelings. After all, he was my cousin and I was supposed to be like his kid brother.

I found a way to gently let go, pretending to rub my nose, but he wouldn't let me get away. I started using my hand to point at different locations, pretending to ask him about what shop used to be in this or that location. Didn't work. In a casual way, he just held on tight to my hand, no matter what I tried to do. He continued giving the tour of the shops, people, and places where we used to hang out and play, and the entire time I was getting weirded out by my cousin trying to hold my hand.

As we walked over to the snack shop, I noticed a handful of others hanging out. As is often the case in India, I didn't see many boys and girls holding hands in public, and it slowly became apparent that my cousin's gesture was a simple sign of affection. He had missed me over the past twenty years, which was evident in his smile, and he couldn't contain his emotion inside.

As we returned to his house, my discomfort completely subsided. I noticed many other men holding hands while crossing the street, walking into shops, or just hanging out and having tea. That day, I learned that it is a societal norm to demonstrate your love, care, and affection for another man, not through hugs or fist bumps but often by simply holding hands.

More importantly, I learned that people in India aren't afraid to share their affection, worries, fears, hopes, or dreams with one another. The social bonds that we build and cultivate, even through simple gestures, are crucial to helping us get through some of the most trying times of our lives. It gives us strength and motivates us to move forward. So it's OK to be pushed outside of your comfort zone and to accept someone else's unique way of showing caring and affection. Really, when you think about it, isn't it a little silly to be stressed out by someone who wants to hold your hand?

PART 2

Don't Overthink

Don't overanalyze. Don't overplan. Don't try to predict the future.

No matter how smart we are, we cannot accurately predict what will happen tomorrow. Life is complicated, interconnected, and intertwined. The world is so complex, growing so fast, that it is impossible to make any reasonable predictions. Having more information doesn't always help. In fact, it can debilitate. Things change constantly. It's fine to think about pros and cons and the consequences of our actions, but too often our minds try to get perfect certainty, and sometimes we get lost in the process.

Let's stop overthinking what other people do, think, or say. Let's realize that love, career, business, the economy, or our future are not predictable. Let's redirect those thoughts toward working on our purpose, our passion, our love, our family, our friends, and our work. Let's rechannel all that overthinking and worrying about tomorrow toward the most certain thing we have in life: our own actions today.

CHAPTER 4

HOW TO CHOOSE A
SPOUSE IN AN HOUR

You can adapt to anything—you just don't
know it yet.

W e're standing there, feet held firmly together, inches away from the water, waiting to jump. So often in life we feel as though we're about to move forward, but something holds us back. It is our own mind. We are afraid of not being able to handle the unpredictable events that may result from a change or a decision we're about to make. Starting a new job, a new relationship, or a new business can seem overwhelming, especially when we've never done it before. Our overly analytical mind tries to protect us by reminding us that we don't have enough information to proceed, that we're not smart enough, that we're not good enough, that we lack something. We may worry that the person we're about to start a relationship with isn't the right one, or we may wonder whether quitting our job will make us really happy. How do we know?

So we worry and think on it some more. We find ourselves getting nervous, anxious, and stressed about jumping in. And that anxiety becomes a vicious cycle, whittling away the time available to pursue our dreams of starting a new relationship, a new business, or a new career; of making a sales call; of pitching a new idea at work; of rebuilding a relationship or starting a fresh life in another place.

About two years ago, I met a young woman named Garima who helped me realize that making a life decision depends not on having more information but on our ability to believe that we can adapt and improvise as we go forward. In our gut, our human intuition, we have an amazingly deep reservoir of strength and the faculty to adjust ourselves to a complex and unpredictable environment—to learn, to develop, to change, to pivot, and to adapt. We can figure things out even when we're flying blind. Improvising is something we don't normally think about, but we know how to do it when we must.

o   o   o

Mallika sent me a Facebook message inviting me to meet her and a couple of her friends for coffee. She wanted to give me a care package for her sister living in New Jersey, and grabbing a coffee was a lot easier than going to her home, because her parents would insist on the lengthy and usually formal dinner. I had been traveling with my boss in India for a work project and my stomach had been through the ups and downs of various foods throughout the last couple of weeks. I just couldn't handle another huge meal.

I arrived a bit early on a brisk and cloudy Saturday morning. The chic coffee place was located in the middle of the touristy, high-end shopping district of New Delhi, and I found myself fascinated by simply observing the ebb and flow of young, modern women going in and out of the fancy shops. Many things had changed since I left this complex country in the late 1970s. Although much of India still lives in poverty, it was refreshing to see the dynamic can-do and must-have spirit of modern India reflected in its bright new shopping centers bustling with energy.

Plush sofas, tall tables, and stools decorated the coffee shop, which was perched atop a tiny building. The aroma of cappuccino was wafting through the air along with the sounds of Beyoncé on the radio.

Mallika arrived with two friends, Garima and Priyanka, who were spending some quality time together later that day. After I received the package from Mallika, we chatted for a bit. We got on the subject of Facebook and how popular it had become in India, especially among young women their age—in their mid- to late twenties—and how the phone call had been replaced by the Facebook message, BlackBerry IM, or text message. I was curious about how the younger generation was finding love in Facebook times, and I inquired as gently as I could into their social lives. In particular, I asked about marriage, thinking that much would have changed since the time of my parents' generation, or even my own.

Offering context, I explained that during my parents' generation, people got married very quickly, without deliberating too long on making a decision. In some cases back then, the couples didn't even meet face-to-face until the day of the wedding. This was especially true for girls. A husband was chosen for them through family acquaintances, and often they were forced into marriage.

In my parents' case, my dad met my mom through relatives who knew my mom's father. My dad went to meet my mom at her parents' home, where she lived. Accompanied by his uncle and aunt, my dad met my mom's parents over tea. My mom brought out tea for all of them and then left to go and hide in the kitchen with her sister, peering out to get a good look at my dad.

The two families had tea together and my dad and mom didn't even exchange a single word. He looked at her briefly and she looked at him. That was it. Tea was over and they left.

Later that evening, my mom's father went over to see my dad and his uncle and promptly asked, "Yes or no?" Talk about pressure!

My dad said yes and they were married in a few weeks' time.

"This was in the late 1960s. How has this changed? What's it like now?" I asked innocently.

"Well, you know, it's harder now because you don't know if you can trust anyone so easily these days," Mallika said. "It used to be that you knew that the boy came from a good family and that was good enough. Nowadays, it's more complicated. Can't be certain of anything anymore. You can't count on the family background, either. In the past, you had some comfort in knowing the boy's family background and so you would think the boy was raised in a good house and he'll make a good husband. But today, you can't count on that anymore." She sounded frustrated.

"It takes more time these days, too," Priyanka chimed in, echoing Mallika's frustration. "A lot of guys are going for higher education now and so they don't want to settle down until they start earning money."

"Or they are so picky!" Garima added, and all of us started laughing.

"What about you, Garima?" I asked.

"I guess I just got lucky," Garima said, beaming a soft smile.

"What do you mean?" I asked.

"I've been married for almost two years now, and it was a chance circumstance. A couple of years ago, my mom wanted me to meet this guy who was ten years older than me. I said, *No way!* I mean, I was only twenty-five years old, and thirty-five seemed like he was an old man, you know?

"Then, about six months later, this guy sent me a message on Facebook, out of the blue. I really didn't remember that it was the same guy, but thought I knew him from school or we had common friends. So we started chatting on Facebook a bit, and a few days later he asked me out for coffee.

"We had a nice time at the coffee shop, and I did remember then that he was ten years older than me, but somehow I didn't notice it. It didn't bother me. I mean, it wasn't love at first sight that you see in a Bollywood movie. I'm not sure it ever is. But we hit it off.

"When he asked me out for a lunch on the second date, I figured, Sure. Why not? He was nice and came from a nice family. We got to the restaurant and we talked about everything—about his idea of pursuing a legal career or higher education, about my pursuit of a master's degree, also. We talked about his father's passing some years ago and how he's managing to take care of his family. We also talked about where in general we wanted to go with our lives."

As Garima was explaining what they talked about, I noticed she didn't mention discussing likes or dislikes.

"Then, at the end of our lunch, he said that he wouldn't have asked me out if he didn't intend on marrying me."

"No! Seriously?" I asked in surprise. "On your second date, this guy essentially asked you to marry him? On your second date? Over lunch? In under an hour, basically?" I wanted to ensure I had heard correctly.

Smiling, Garima answered, "Well, I guess so. He took me by surprise. I was shocked too."

"What did you say?"

"I said OK. Yes. I mean, I knew I wanted a good family, someone with good education, must be decent looking and have some connection. But also nothing was final, of course, since he hadn't met my family and they had not met him either."

Mallika and Priyanka both said, "The family plays more of a role in our decision making."

Priyanka explained further, "Knowing that the boy comes from a good family usually indicates that he's a good boy. And if Garima's parents didn't like him, then she may not have married him."

"My parents had some knowledge of his family, all through the perspective of people we knew in common," Garima added.

This is getting interesting, I thought. I asked, "But you still had final say, right? Then what happened?"

"Well, he came over my house to meet my parents, and that was it. They liked him and we decided to get married. But I kind of knew on our first date," she said confidently.

"But help me understand something. How did you know he's the one?" I asked, almost teasingly.

Without feeling the pressure of trying to explain a decision that lasts a lifetime, Garima explained her rationale with almost philosophical ease.

"Just because you don't have a negative vibe when you're on a date or a lunch, it doesn't mean that you won't ever fight or argue in the future or have difficult times in your marriage. Because I understand that life is never easy."

She paused to allow her friends to nod in agreement, their body language becoming that of women with far more years behind them.

"There are always compromises in any relationships," she continued. "But you know what? We'll make it work. We will figure it out. We'll learn as we go. We'll make it work!"

As we ended our fun, rich, and deep conversation amid pastries and lattes on a rainy Saturday in India's new urban metropolis, I realized that some things don't change. Although parts of India's landscape may appear changed on the surface, its citizens' deep reservoir of acceptance for the imperfections of life hadn't changed all that much since the day my parents met some four decades ago.

I realized that, along with the package I was bringing back for Mallika's sister, I was taking back a lesson that I needed to apply to my own life.

There is no special knowledge that surrounds the decision of a young woman to go forward with a lifelong decision to marry a man she has met for only an hour or so. Whether Garima's marriage will work out cannot be known for certain. What is important, however, is her strong belief in the ability to *make* it work, a belief that comes from an acceptance that life has its ups and downs and that there is no perfect life, person, relationship, or marriage. Instead of certainty, Garima has steadfast faith in her own ability to figure it out as she goes. She has faith in her ability—in *their* ability—to be fluid, flexible, and agile as life unfolds; to improvise; to be secure in an insecure world, armed with only the knowledge that resilience exists within. And part of this is due to Garima's ability to not overthink.

CHAPTER 5

CELEBRATING A BIRTHDAY WITH NOTHING BUT A BOLLYWOOD SONG

You already have the important things in life.

Many of us struggle to balance tasks that make us happy with tasks that provide financial support for our family. Some even argue that we have to do this or that so that we may have things that provide comfort, which in turn will likely provide us with happiness. It's a challenge I have struggled with myself, especially during our recent economic uncertainty.

However, I learned a valuable lesson while my wife, three-year-old daughter, and I were visiting my cousin and his family a few years ago. While we were celebrating a birthday with a Bollywood song and cake in a tiny apartment on the outskirts of India's most congested city, I realized that happiness is not expensive. We struggle to find things that make us happy and keep us going, but sometimes these things are not found at the mall or on some far-off tropical island. Instead, they are right in front of us.

o   o   o

Friday evening rush hour in New Delhi is one of the worst times to travel, given the sheer number of cars, scooters, motorcycles, and whatever else is escorting passengers to the most popular destination in the world: home. Thick smog, fog, and plain old fumes descended upon us as, one Friday at dusk, we began our journey from one end of New Delhi to the other to visit my cousin's family.

I was stressed about packing in the morning for the trip back to the United States, anxious to get home, and tired from the long week, and I wasn't in the mood to sit through a bunch of traffic. This trip to my cousin's place, to check on the family and see if they were OK, was something I had promised my dad I would do.

My wife and daughter had fallen asleep after the first hour of traffic and I was starting to doze off during the second leg. Amid the humming of scooters and the blowing of horns, I drifted off to sleep, thinking about the last time I saw my cousin, Rakesh, about fifteen years before.

At the time, he had just gotten married and was going to bring his entire family from the village where he grew up to New Delhi, where he was starting to make a new life as a tailor.

Rakesh's first try at New Delhi came at the age of seventeen, when he left his mom, his two sisters, and a younger brother to seek out a job in the big city. Having lost his father at the age of eleven, he grew up fast, taking on the responsibility of caring for his mother and siblings. But there was no work to be found in the village, so his aunt suggested that he come to Delhi, where she had found him a job with a car mechanic and he could learn the trade.

He tried to become a car mechanic, learned a lot, and was getting secure enough in his job to bring the rest of his family to Delhi. But then the accident happened. A car he was working on fell on him. He was badly injured and lost part of his right index finger. Scared, scarred, and defeated, he went back to his village.

After a year of bouncing between jobs and trying to feed his family in the village, he became desperate. This time, an uncle invited him back to Delhi to train as a tailor in the uncle's shop. Through pricks of the needle, hunger in the stomach, and the fear of not being able to feed his family back in the village, Rakesh learned to measure, cut, and sew. He grew in his trade by working for a year in the back room of his uncle's shop, which was more like a cave, making men's suits, women's clothing, and children's school uniforms late into the night.

When we left him that year, I was feeling very sorry for him. He was my blood, and although he was a few years older, I wanted to take care of him, even though in those days my own family was struggling to survive in the United States. I gave him whatever money I had, some $800. It wasn't much, but it was what I had brought to India.

I didn't know how he was going to earn a living as a tailor when there seemed to be tailors on every corner. How would he feed his extended family? Where would they live? He had a younger brother, a mother, a wife, a younger sister, and an older sister with a depressed husband and a newborn baby girl. How the heck was he going to take care of all of them by himself when he was just learning to sew clothes?

I didn't know how to help him except to give him money. But how much was enough?

My mind was filled with worry for him when I awoke from my nap to the voice of our driver, who was asking me for further directions.

We finally arrived at Rakesh's apartment complex around 8 p.m. Our car approached a set of five-story buildings with poor lighting, situated on congested, narrow back streets filled with carts selling all sorts of snacks. Yellow lanterns hanging on a makeshift snack shops lit the way as we finally located an unmarked building we could barely tell was inhabited.

Our taxi driver turned to the corner of the building and found a tight parking spot between a sleeping cow and some motorcycles. He agreed to wait for us while we had dinner. We used the light from our cell phones to find our way up the stairs to the tiny apartment.

The fifth-floor apartment was small. We sat huddled together in his living room, which contained a small sofa, a couple of old tables, and a handful of folding chairs. Surrounded by the extended family, who seemed overwhelmed with joy to have us visit, we felt a bit like museum pieces on display. My daughter, who had never met her Indian cousins, got a little scared and clung to her mother.

Slowly, the girls and women in the family brought out glasses of water on a tray, with snacks to munch on while dinner was being prepared. Amid the wonderful aroma of the dinner cooking in the tiny kitchen, we started to feel the warmth of their offerings, the kind way they suggested that we eat . . . and eat . . . and eat.

With a smile that had seen lots of pain and suffering, Rakesh explained how he had fared over the previous few years. He seemed to be doing well in his work and business.

"Aren't you worried about competition from China and *all* the orders that are heading there?" I asked.

Deep down, he was probably as scared about an uncertain future as anyone, but with a wink he said, "I don't need all the orders. Just one."

Since I had last seen him, he had brought his entire family over from the village and started out on his own. Living and working out of a tiny one-bedroom apartment with his extended family, most sleeping on blankets on the floor, he began a business of making school uniforms. Getting a school contract to sell uniforms was not easy, but over a few years he managed to get a contract here and there, and he just kept at it. He got his younger brother to go out and procure more contracts from schools and his business grew. They soon managed to save some money and got a bigger apartment, which still served as both home and workplace for them and their three employees, who slept in makeshift housing on the roof of their building.

While Rakesh and I were chatting about his journey with work and business, I watched his two sons and two nieces go over, pick up my daughter, and start playing with her. It felt great to see their sheer delight with their little American cousin. They played with her, wanted her to eat chocolate, and showed her all the things they had around, including a torn old black-and-white photo of me as a baby.

In showing my daughter photos of her dad in younger years, it seemed they were trying to foster an understanding that we were all the same. However distant we might live, we were still the same blood. We were family.

Dinner was served with great affection, warmth, and care, and everyone's eyes were on my wife, my daughter, and me to make sure we didn't have any need that went unnoticed.

After a meal that was as rich in butter as hospitality and love, Rakesh's wife brought out a small cake with seven candles on it to celebrate her son's seventh birthday. With his older brother and four other cousins joking around him, Rakesh's son blew out the candles. He was a slim boy, wearing nothing but torn slippers and a blue long sleeve shirt with vertical stripes. According to custom, everyone took turns feeding the birthday boy a little piece of cake, symbolic of gifts that have a more lasting meaning than something purchased at a store.

Then Rakesh's older son, age eleven, brought out the latest Bollywood music. All the kids broke out in dance and sang along. The rhythm of the song transported them to the hills of the Swiss Alps, where so many Bollywood films find their backdrop. They were in heaven. They sang, they danced, they showed us a few moves.

The melody was uplifting but also melancholic, and it brought back my worried look and my concerns about Rakesh's ability to find financial security in the future. I asked him, "Rakesh, do you need anything? Can I help you in any way?" I didn't want to offend him by talking about money, but I wanted to let him know that I was there for him.

Casually rubbing the remnants of his lost index finger, Rakesh eased further into his chair, beaming his smile as he looked around the room. Full of happiness, joy, and cake, his family celebrated, joking around with one another, laughing at little things, dancing. My wife and daughter joined the dance in the middle of the tiny room, lit up by the family's smiles.

Rakesh paused and looked back at me, not with the eyes of a desperate man who was unsure where his next meal was coming from but with the eyes of one who was at peace despite the problems at his doorstep. With a deep smile, he said, "Thanks, but this is all I really need. Isn't it?"

His words hit me at the core of my being, and as my eyes started to well up I responded, "You're right, my brother. This *is* all we really need. Happiness of our kids dancing to a Bollywood song, celebrating life with a birthday cake."

I was well aware that he was still struggling financially, but that was OK for him because he had something more important.

Our departure was around midnight and lasted an hour as we stood around the car hugging, smiling, and promising to stay connected. As our daughter drifted off to sleep on the drive back, my wife and I looked at each other with joyful tears and realized that what we had felt in that tiny apartment was a pure moment of joy, brought on by nothing more than a family gathering over Bollywood music and a birthday cake.

My cousin was truly living his life, despite the seemingly overwhelming challenges he faced each day. He moved forward with nothing more than the family that surrounded him, affection, and the occasional celebration. They put food on the handful of plates they owned and got through it with an attitude that was hopeful and carefree.

I realized that moments of joy are not necessarily found in the crockery surrounding the cake but in the tiny celebrations of life with family, friends, and a Bollywood song.

CHAPTER 6

MISSING THE DANCE AT
AN INDIAN WEDDING

Worrying about what's coming next will
make you miss the best times of your life.

Sometimes we get so lost in overthinking the future that we forget to live in the here and now and we risk missing the best times of our lives. Some of the best ideas, greatest people, most wonderful relationships, and best times can emerge during times of chaos.

Some years ago, my wife and I went to India to see her only brother get married. I had been to Indian weddings in the United States, but it wasn't enough to prepare me for one of the most chaotic but memorable experiences I've ever had.

An Indian wedding is an event where people run in all different directions, where time has no meaning, and where horses, strange uncles, and even the bride show up out of nowhere. At the wedding, I was trying too hard to control, to force my own logical, orderly, and boxed way of thinking onto something that is completely unpredictable. I learned a lot about myself that day and have since realized that I never again want to miss the moment in front of me by allowing my mind to focus so much on what's next.

○ ○ ○

"What do you mean the horse isn't here?" I said to one of the many cousins and friends lurking around the grandmother's house as we were getting ready for the big night. My brother-in-law, who lives in the United States, was getting married to a woman from India, in her home city of New Delhi.

I had only been to one other wedding in India, and I was sick with "Delhi belly" at the time, so I don't recollect much of anything except the side of the road where my food often ended up. Besides, this time was different. As the oldest, sane, and organized American, I was kind of in charge . . . or so I thought.

In an Indian wedding, the bride's side of the family usually sends a horse to pick up the groom on the evening of the wedding. Adorned by flowers and fed by the boy's sisters, the horse is supposed to carry the groom slowly alongside the *bandwala* (traveling band) guys and the rest of the groom's party in a procession to the location of the ceremony. But neither the horse nor the band were anywhere to be found.

"*Are you kidding me?*" I started screaming, when my wife informed me that she still had to go to the hair salon to get her hair and makeup done. "We were supposed to have left an hour ago and there's no horse, no band, and the groom's sister isn't ready. What is the deal with everyone? Why can't we ever get this stuff right? Don't they know it's the wedding day?"

No one was listening. My wife had left for the hair salon. The rest were busy doing whatever it is people do in India before a wedding.

Chicken.

No head.

I was exhausted from three days of events, functions, food, and formalities—a slew of pre-wedding parties that all seemed to blend in with each other. It was all too much, and at this point I was eager to get it over with. The stress and anxiety of being in India for two weeks—and of using two-thirds of my precious vacation time from work—was getting to me.

As I stood outside in the cold evening air, waiting, I wondered why they couldn't do a destination wedding in a normal place like Florida or Cancún, like other people.

The groom's dad was out running an errand (seriously, who runs an errand at such a time?), and the groom's mom was freaking out, trying to prepare gifts, envelopes, jewelry, flowers, sweets, and all the rest of the items required as part of the inventory of things exchanged between the bride's and groom's families. She had no time to worry about a horse.

And there's never a dress rehearsal. So off I went to take charge, because it felt like everything was falling apart and someone needed to take charge. After figuring out who had ordered the horse, I tried to get in touch with the horse guy. No answer. Called the *bandwala* guys. No answer. Finally, I went outside to get some air and took a walk around the neighborhood in hopes of perhaps finding the horse, who may have gotten lost.

And there he was. The horse! And the horse's handler, just sitting on a stack of bricks near a construction site on the side of the street.

"What are you doing? Why aren't you at the house? Come on. Let's go."

"Yes, sir," he said, rising.

But he just stood there, smiling and shaking his head.

"Why don't you move?" I asked. "Let's go. We are getting late."

"Yes, sir." Still just standing there.

"What is the problem, man?" I asked in great frustration.

"Sir, you have such a big house and we are such little people . . ."

Are you kidding me? Was this guy trying to shake me down for some more money simply because he's got me in my time of need? So typical! And this wasn't even my house!

I stopped him right there.

"Don't worry about the money. I'll take care of you." This assured him enough to start walking.

Horse. Check. I felt relieved. Things were going my way.

Thank God I'm here, I thought. Otherwise this wedding would fall apart. The control-freak ego was rearing its ugly head.

Next, the traveling band.

As I walked back to the house with the horse and his handler, I was relieved to see that the bandwalas had also arrived. Thank God! The band was about a dozen Indian men, dressed in white, Westernized band uniforms that were clearly aged to perfection by the crisp, roasted streets of New Delhi. They had probably picked them up at some Army/Navy store, if there was such a thing in India. Some were holding instruments—tubas, trumpets, or drums. The others held up candelabra-type lighting powered by portable generators.

My wife finally arrived from the hair salon and we were finally ready to go. We were arguing because she's "always" late and I am a stickler for time.

"Can we finally go now? Which car are we taking?" I asked.

"We can't leave yet," she answered. "We have to get him on the horse."

"I know, but that's for the photos, right? I mean, he's not going to ride that horse all the way to the hotel. . . . Is he?"

"I don't know, babe," she responded, and then she was pulled away by giggling girls.

"What happens next?" I asked my wife's father.

"They feed the horse," he responded, almost sarcastically, probably because he figured I would know how Indian weddings go, having been married in an Indian wedding in the United States.

I couldn't help feeling a little foolish. I mean, I kind of knew what was going on, but it felt so different. My own Indian American wedding some years ago in New Jersey was a little tamer than this. I had done what I was told to do and just smiled and waved. It was all such a blur.

And the wedding invitation didn't say anything about feeding a horse.

The procession of young girl cousins, friends, and my wife ceremoniously fed the horse, which had been further adorned everywhere with flowers and symbols. The groom, all dressed up with his flower helmet, his necklace of rupees, and his very manly customary sword, climbed up on the horse and, accompanied by a beating drum, began his journey toward that holy alliance, marriage.

"Good photos. What's next?" I asked innocently.

Off we went. But not as I expected.

The groom, high on top of his horse, followed a procession of his family and friends—some walking and some dancing—down the streets of New Delhi to the site of the marriage ceremony, a few miles away. Lit by the weak glow of light rods blurred by the mist in the cold winter air, the procession looked worn, tired. The procession was going slowly and we had a long way to go. They weren't going to make it.

My stomach started to churn and the pressure was building in my mind as I looked at my watch and realized that we were about two hours behind. Something about time always makes me nervous. I like to be on time. No, I *need* to be on time. I was trained in sales, and in my mind I could hear the voice of a former New York City sales manager from twenty years ago: "Be early, but never, ever be late."

I popped some pink tablets that were supposedly Pepto-Bismol, but the spelling was wrong, so I knew they were knockoffs. Whatever. I needed to calm my stomach. If only they made that stuff for my head, I thought.

I had joined the procession and was walking along with my wife and the rest of the family. I told my wife we weren't going to make it in time and suggested that we go a few yards forward with the half-dancing procession, and then all of us could get in the cars that were following us and head over to the venue. The band could get there in the van that was accompanying them. That left the horse, which could probably gallop to the venue. Why not? It is India, after all. I figured we would have time to do all the dancing in the parking lot before the *milni*, the official meeting of the two families.

This seemed reasonable enough to my wife, her brother the groom, and their parents, who all agreed. I didn't want to further our argument about why my wife was so late, so I got into a car with a bunch of "uncles" who were part of the wedding procession. They weren't my uncles, literally, but in

India you address anyone relatively older than you as uncle or auntie, out of respect. Six of us were squeezed into the car.

As soon as I entered the car, I felt much better, more relaxed. At least were moving in the right direction, toward our destination.

We went a few miles and then the uncle in the front seat asked the driver to stop the car on the side of the road. It was not a major road, only one of the side roads, but it was still a fairly busy street, in the evening after rush hour. The uncle got out of the car and the others started to follow. The van carrying the band had kept up with us pretty well and pulled over to the side of the road ahead of us.

What now? I wondered. We were probably only half a mile away, but we were still a good two hours late.

Stressed and anxious to get there already, I unwillingly got out of the car with the others to see what was going on. One of the uncles went behind the car and opened the trunk. I figured he had forgotten something. Curious, I went over to see what he was getting out.

"You gotta be kidding me!" I couldn't help saying it aloud. It just came out. In the trunk of the car, in plain sight, was a big cooler full of ice and four or five bottles of scotch. "You got out to get some Johnnie Walker?" I asked in amazement.

"Want some?" he asked, smiling as he started to pour.

I guess the open trunk of a white Maruti Suzuki behind a wedding procession of *bandwala* guys in dirty white uniforms is a smoke signal of some kind, indicating to all the men attending a wedding, "Bar is open for business! Come and get it!" All of a sudden, three or four other cars in our party started lining up behind ours.

Some of the other guests were bringing out their own preferred single malts, along with some salted snacks. One of the uncles brought out some roasted almonds and started passing them around in a paper cup. There they were, standing in the middle of the road in a major Indian city, drinking Johnnie Walker Black Label out of the trunk of some uncle's car, heading to the wedding of my brother-in-law, with a traveling band in front of us—two hours late.

My neck became stiff and I was freaking out.

In hindsight, I could probably have used the drink, but I refused. It didn't correlate with my view of how things were supposed to be. I couldn't drink on the side of a road with all these cars passing by!

I implored the handful of uncles to get back in the car. Their only response was, "Relax. Come on, have a drink. We'll get there. Don't worry about it. Have a little fun. Besides, he *will* get married."

Tension continued to creep into my body as I stood, amazed, watching these uncles shooting the breeze as if they were having a backyard barbeque. I've been to plenty of tailgate parties in a parking lot before a football game, but we were late for a wedding! How could anyone be so relaxed?

The procession of women dressed in beautiful saris arrived in their cars, bit by bit filling the black-and-white scene with vibrant colors, bringing life to what felt like a circus where no one was taking anything seriously. Soon, there was a row of cars parked on the side of the road, one in front of the other.

My worry increased as the other women in the wedding procession began pouring out of their cars. With my wife leading the way, they headed over to the band and the drumbeat began in full force. Everyone started dancing spontaneously. Their sore feet were infused with a burst of energy, laying claim to the big fat Indian wedding *bhangra* music. Tired faces were brought back to life, smiling, rejoicing in a celebration that comes once in a lifetime.

My wife was loving it. She peered over at me, winked, smiled, and started dancing, signaling for me to come over and join her. Her spontaneous wink broke my stiff demeanor, but I still couldn't let go. The time pressure to get there made me resist her invitation to dance. I needed to get everyone there. I felt responsible because I felt like no one was in charge. The uncles were laughing, enjoying their Black Label. The women, in their rich, vibrantly colored saris, sparkling jewelry, and extravagant shoes, were dancing with some of the younger male family members.

I considered what I would be doing right now back home. How different this looked from my daily routine view of black and blue coats rushing to grab bagels and coffee. There was something about the colors, vibrant hues dancing all around, celebrating with open arms, inviting me to join in on the fun. But I still couldn't get myself to let go. To liberate myself from the shackles of my notions of how things ought to be. To be free and just dance.

Deep inside, I wanted to join in, but my overthinking wouldn't allow me to be free of this self-imposed responsibility to get to the wedding on time. I wanted to dance with my wife, but I couldn't. Conflicting thoughts in my head wanted me to maintain my almost Western composure. I couldn't accept the chaos. And I felt as if I was suffering for it.

Slowly, the band started walking forward to the venue, along with the procession of dancing women—now joined by boisterous husbands who had at last found their confidence.

Finally! We arrived at the parking lot of the hotel where the wedding was supposed to take place. My stress lifted when I realized that we had gotten there.

A number of the bride's family members were gathered on the platform where the groom and bride were supposed to formally meet each other. I felt embarrassed at being so late and went up to check in with one of the bride's many cousins, to say hello and to apologize. To my shock and surprise, I learned that the bride was just getting there herself.

"Oh, man. No way. You have to be kidding me. I give up."

Exhaling a breath of exasperation, I sat down on the platform to wait another twenty minutes or so, chatting with some of the bride's cousins. In some ways, I couldn't help laughing a little.

The bride arrived in all her beautiful glory. Amid music and much fanfare, the bride and groom exchanged their formal flower necklaces. The array of family members exchanged red envelopes and gifts. This went on for a good half hour.

Escorted inside, the bride and groom walked side by side to a platform adorned with soft cushions and flowers. Seated next to the pandit who would be performing the marriage ceremony, they smiled nervously. Sitting across from a small, square block of bricks where the fire would eventually burn, the pandit began the ceremony.

Over the course of the next two hours, the pandit performed the ceremony, sometimes in Hindi and often in the ancient Indian language of Sanskrit, while the couple faced the fire. Pouring oil, wood, and other earthly materials into the fire, the couple repeated their holy vows and sought blessings from God. With all the families sitting around smiling at the young couple, blessings of love, affection, and excitement continued to flow throughout the night.

In what I would have thought to be a more serious part of the ceremony, some young guys were casually joking around behind the groom. Girls were also in a playful mood as they hatched their plans to play a joke on the groom after the ceremony. Something about stealing his shoes and then making him buy them back. Giving the young guys a serious stare, I hoped they would chill out and let the pandit perform.

It was all so confusing at times. Some people were praying, some were laughing, some were dozing off, others were intensely focused on the burning pyre.

Eventually, the pandit tied the groom's coattails to the bride's red sari and they walked around the fire seven times. Watching the young couple's faces as they walked around the small, warm fire put me into something of a peaceful trance. It had been a long day. And it was over. That was it.

They were married.

Following many more fun and vivacious rituals and customs—including the new husband buying his shoes back from his bride's girlfriends—we ate our dinner, which lasted late into the night.

"What happened to the dancing?" I asked my wife.

"That's it. No more dancing," she said, turning her attention back to her kid brother who had just become a married man.

Everyone sat around a table enjoying one another's company until 2 or 3 a.m. I was relieved that the wedding had taken place and everything went fine and everyone was happy. I felt satisfied but not fulfilled. Relieved but not happy. I couldn't believe it was actually over, but I felt like something was missing.

It went by so fast, I thought. My heart felt as though I had unfinished business. I wanted to celebrate, to dance. But it was all out of order. You're supposed to dance after they get married, not before. That was it. They got it wrong. It's all upside down here. How are you supposed to celebrate something that hasn't finished yet?

As we were leaving the hotel to go back to the house, exhausted, I glanced over at the still-burning fire, and suddenly I realized that *they* had not gotten it wrong. *I* had gotten it wrong. I was so focused on the destination that I forgot to enjoy the ride. I was worried about the wrong things. My mind had been so busy focusing on my way of thinking about how things ought to be that I didn't enjoy how things really were. I was so worried about getting to the wedding on time and what was coming next that I didn't fully enjoy the experience of the horse, the cocktails by the side of the road, dancing with my beautiful, joyful wife, the rituals and customs and their deep meaning.

I didn't appreciate the ride, but ultimately it all ends the same way: two people get married. They get married, and everything works out in the end. My overthinking mind had made me miss possibly some of the best moments of my life. This was my wife's only brother, and I had missed out on dancing at his wedding.

Exhausted as I was, the picture of the trip was still vibrantly alive in my mind as we flew home the next day. I was deep in thought and didn't realize the flight attendant was asking me if I wanted any water.

My wife joked, "He's still thinking about my brother's wedding we just came from."

With a sparkle in her eye, the flight attendant replied, "They're great aren't they? I just absolutely love Indian weddings! All that jewelry, colors, smells, food—and the dancing! And the shoe negotiations at the end! I miss it, too."

Perhaps sensing my disappointment and regret, my wife gave my arm a little squeeze.

"Don't worry, honey," the flight attendant added. "There's always an Indian wedding happening somewhere in the world."

CHAPTER 7

LEARNING TO MEDITATE
AMID CHAOS

Daily rituals serve to remind us to start
participating in life.

Each day a billion Indians, from poor farmers to Bombay billionaires, rise in the morning and awaken to complicated, chaotic lives. Before they leave their homes, however, they undertake a ritual that has been practiced for generations before them and will likely be followed by those who come after. They fold their hands in prayer, yielding their lives to the universe. Doing so is a recognition that much of their lives is not determined by their own will but by a force greater than themselves.

For many Indians, the day's travels will also take them to an Indian temple. Indians do not banish chaos at the doors of most holy places—actually, in a sense, they expect it. There is so much confusion at an Indian temple. So many gods. So many people doing different things. Take off your shoes. Wash your hands. Ring the bell. Spill this water over this particular statue. Put a flower on the feet of that statue. The divine fragrance of incense intoxicates the mind while the ears take in the sounds of a schoolgirl's whispered prayers and the ringing bells indicating that another worshipper has entered in search of solace.

Bells, incense—it's all so much, so confusing. There's so much noise that you can't meditate. You can't think straight. All the random thoughts about tomorrow that you entered with are drowned out by the noise, the smells, and the visual assortment. So many senses are being evoked that there's no room for contemplative prayer.

Even the pandits don't give you time to think. Instead, they make you move.

Amid all the confusion and these complicated methods of reaching God, however, you are forced to stop thinking about the bills, the problems at work, or the uncertain future that is yet to materialize. Instead, you are encouraged to start participating. You move your hands, sing, say verses in ancient Sanskrit, which you don't understand.

Move your feet. Ring a bell. Throw flowers. Pour milk. Fold your hands. Say "Om."

You can't think. You *do*.

And that's the point. It's moving meditation.

I've realized that Indian temples are not there to provide the teachings of God so that you have the answers to all the questions in your life. They serve a more practical purpose, as a reminder that, just as your heart is moving and brings life beat by beat, you are living by actively doing. Living in the present moment is the path to the divinity all around you. While you are pursuing, chasing, walking, running, breathing, working, and engaging, you have a life worth living, right here and right now.

o o o

Stop at almost any traffic light in India and you can't help noticing the bells ringing from the Hindu temples scattered everywhere. On major roads, in the middle of village corn-fields, in back streets, and everywhere in between, Hindu temples delight the senses even as they offer a rich architec-tural offering to the gods.

In the New Jersey suburbs of the 1980s, there was only one Hindu temple nearby, and I had been there many times while growing up, mainly because of my mom's deep reli-gious beliefs. Every Tuesday—and occasionally Saturday or Sunday—became our family's time to reconnect with our creator and the small number of Indian families making their way in America. Familiarity with a Hindu temple in the United States, however, didn't prepare me adequately for visiting one in India.

One morning in New Delhi, slowly recovering from jet lag, I rose from my bed really early. From the small window of my cousin's house, I looked out at the cows freely roam-ing the back street, looking for breakfast in the heaps of gar-bage spread everywhere. I also noticed a number of scooters beginning to fill the crowded area of what looked like the parking lot of the local Hindu temple.

I had been in India for a few days and the cold in the house was getting to me. How can they have no heaters in the house? What's the deal with this thin little blanket? I felt angry about everything that seemed out of place. Why is this here? Why is that over there? I just wanted to check into a hotel to find some comfort in a predictable and seemingly safe place where things would be as I wanted them to be.

I had left my wife and kids back home and was feeling a bit guilty for coming out to attend another wedding. There also were changes happening at work, and I felt that if I wasn't in the office I was missing out on something important. In fact, anxiety about the future of my job, the company, and the economic environment had disturbed my sleep more than the jet lag. I had a brain freeze and couldn't figure the future out, and I was feeling as if I really didn't need to be in India because I was spending so much time thinking about what was going on back home.

Partly because I needed to get some "fresh" air and partly because I was curious about the scooters at the temple, I decided to get out and see why so many people were gathering so early on a Tuesday morning. I walked over, hoping to find someone getting married or someone announcing the birth of a child. Or perhaps, in some subconscious way, I was trying to reach out to God to help me with my own problems. Couldn't hurt, right?

Nothing special was going on that day. No wedding, no funeral. It was a typical Tuesday morning, when lots of worshippers drop in before heading to work, opening their shops, or going to the market.

As I approached the temple, I noticed an older woman using a broom with intense calm to clean the dirt outside. I questioned her progress, because she only moved the dirt from one spot to another. I thought she must be in meditation. Temples in India are really old, always reminding the worshiper that no matter how strong or divine you think you are, you eventually turn to dust.

As I approached the temple, I noticed a collage of shoes littered in front of the entrance, along with a nearby tap used for hand washing. You take off your shoes before entering the temple, and if you use your hands to untie your laces, you must then wash your hands to rinse off the dirt you may have picked up. It's not a precise custom, given the shortage of water in many places throughout India, but the goal is to purify your hands before you touch God.

Inside the temple, I got in some sort of line and did as others do when entering a temple: I rang the bell hanging above me as loud as I could. I always thought it was sort of strange to have such a loud sound at a place where you're supposed to be in prayer.

Walking barefoot onto the cold, wet floor of a local temple brought me to the same level as all the other worshippers seeking answers, strength, and a little help. Man, that floor is cold!

Inside the small temple, there was so much to see that my eyes couldn't really focus on one thing. Many statues of different gods, some small and some large, were placed throughout, with no order. Ganesha with his elephant trunk. Shiva with his blue skin and the famous snake around his neck. The couple Rama and Sita with their monkey-man follower. And God in his own right, Hanuman.

A handful of pandits helped the early-morning worshippers perform prayers of gratitude and requests for prosperity. I observed with keen interest the performance of a man in his forties. He was a little overweight and his graying hair was dyed with henna, which gave him an auburn look. He was with his mother, and it looked as if they might be there to mark the anniversary of the passing of his father, a common Indian practice. The pandit, comfortably seated with his back to the statue of God, was guiding the man and his mother through their rituals.

Another, younger man was there with his mother and father, getting a bit of divine boost for an exam that day. A young woman, her sister, and her mother were perhaps praying for an early wedding. From policemen to businesspeople to teachers and retired civil servants, the temple was filled with worshippers who folded their hands in humility and hope.

Then the pandit turned to me and started to walk me through the rituals, which I originally had no intention of performing. But something inside me just went with it in the hopes that it might help.

Take the marigold flower and break off a piece and put it in front of Ganesha.

Take the holy water from this small bottle brought all the way from the Ganges and pour it over this statue.

Hold this *diya* (candle) and move it around this way.

Touch the feet of this statue of God and say the following words in Sanskrit.

The pandit lit incense and moved around the statue, then he moved over to me to give me the fragrance while I held my hands in prayer.

Take milk and pour it over a stone in the center of another statue, called the *shivling*.

The pandit finished his task by putting a red powdered *bindi* (dot) on my forehead and grabbing my right hand to tie a red thread around my wrist.

By the time he was finished, I was in total confusion. But I went with the flow and did what the pandit told me to do.

My reward was a round, sweet, butter-filled pastry called *prashad*. Like most sweet things in India, it is really, really sweet, and I loved it.

I wasn't sure what else to do, so I walked out of the temple and started putting on my shoes, feeling that the dirt on my mind had been washed away, along with my troubles.

As I began to walk back to the house, my shoulders felt less heavy and my neck was less stiff. Each step I took gave me a little more momentum. The warmth of the winter sun was so inviting that I lifted my face to the sky, taking it in deeply. It seemed to shine in all its glory, bathing the cows that lay about, carefree, probably after finding their morning meal delivered by one of the worshippers coming out of the temple.

My breath was slow and deep and I could feel the presence of all the things around me, as if the earth's rotation had slowed just for me. I heard a dog bark at a cow for stealing his sitting spot. The tiny bells on the rickshaw passing by seemed to be chiming in unison with the beating of my heart. My feelings no longer asleep, I felt each moment. Everything was so clear, and the loneliness of the troubles kicking around in my mind folded into the step, bell, and movement of a greater purpose yet to be revealed.

Going through the motions forced upon me by the pandit had made my mind stop overthinking about the future and had helped to kick-start movement in my feet, turning it into motion and ultimately momentum. Looking down at the red thread on my wrist, I couldn't help but smile, and I found a certain rhythmic spring in my step, in harmony with the locals around me as I kept walking forward.

PART 3

Move Forward

Somehow, in some cosmically random way,
things have a way of working out in the end.
So go ahead; embrace the chaos.

Seeds of inner confidence start to bloom the moment you
stop overthinking and start doing. Taking action is your only
certainty. Get working on what you can do, right here and
right now.

Start putting your purpose to work. If you don't know how, get
out and try something. Throw yourself into a specific cause.
You're more likely to find your purpose when you bring value to
others.

Get moving on what you can control: your actions. You are still
in charge of you. Observe your own thoughts. Focus on your
own actions. Say yes. Try anything. Participate. Dig deep. Get
out of the house. You've been taking chances your whole life;
why stop now? Love. Live. Work. Do.

You'll start feeling better almost immediately because you'll feel
as if you have control again. You'll be in charge of you again
and you'll be on your way . . . somewhere. It's better than sitting
around and waiting for something to happen. Instead, make
things happen.

Life is up, down, good, great, and every way in between . . . and it is short! In a chaotic environment, the walls around us are malleable, offering great opportunities for success and happiness if you jump in and adapt. You just have to move forward.

CHAPTER 8

HITCHHIKING TO WORK
IN MUMBAI

Focusing on your own actions moves you
through the distractions.

Sometimes we feel stuck because there seems to be too much to do in any day. Families rush through breakfast, rush to school, rush to beat the traffic to work, then deal with all the boss's demands. Will we make the 6:45 train home or have to wait another hour and miss dinner? How did we forget to call Mom and Dad last week? What about the prescription that's been waiting at the pharmacy for two days? Why did I ever volunteer to be a soccer coach for the kids on Saturday? I can't believe I have to pay that parking ticket when I was just running in to the dry cleaner for two minutes . . . And then one day you look at your child, your spouse, or yourself in the mirror and realize that twenty years have raced by.

With distractions and challenges around every corner, it's easy to feel as if we're running around a hamster wheel and getting nowhere. How can we fit in more risks, adventures, and unknowns when our plate already seems overflowing? We've all been there.

But my goal in this chapter is to take away your excuses for feeling overloaded. I'll introduce you to a man with an impossible commute, a nearly impossible job, and only one day off each week. Working for a day alongside this sales representative in India's busiest and likely most complex city helped me realize how important it is to have a purpose, to serve others, and to keep moving forward.

o   o   o

Tushar was waiting for me at 9:45 a.m., as he had promised. I found him in the lobby of my hotel, among a handful of men with cell phones attached to their ears. I introduced myself, put out my hand, and received the soft handshake that I had gotten used to receiving from so many in India.

I had spent a few weeks in the field in 1997, riding along with a sales rep in India, and I was excited by the chance to do it again. I wanted to see what it was like to be a sales rep in our modern times in one of the most complex and challenging areas of India—Mumbai.

With a population of more than 20 million people, Mumbai is a city like no other. It's the financial capital of India, the home of Bollywood and billionaires, but also has some of the world's biggest slums. Given the city's diverse, overcrowded, complex culture and its dilapidated infrastructure, it seemed like the perfect place to see modern India collide with old India amid chaos.

"Thank you for allowing me the opportunity to spend the day with you in the field, Tushar. I really appreciate it," I said. I politely waited for his reply, but he shook his head and smiled. To fill the silence while we were waiting for the car to come around to the front of the hotel, I made some small talk.

"How long did it take you to get here? I know that Mumbai traffic is pretty bad in the morning, and especially on a Monday. Do you live far from here?"

Casually, he responded, "Not far. About fifteen kilometers. It took me about two hours to get here."

Shocked, and feeling a little guilty that it took him so long to get to the hotel, I suggested a cup of tea or coffee in the lobby before we proceeded to the field. He declined, saying that he'd had his breakfast at home.

We proceeded to the revolving door of the hotel and went outside to wait for the rental car and driver. Because he was a sales rep for a pharmaceutical company, I assumed Tushar had a company scooter or something, so I asked him where he would leave his scooter while we were meeting with his customers in the field.

"I don't have a scooter, sir. Company doesn't give us a car or a scooter."

"So how did you get here?" I asked in amazement.

With a smile, he answered, "I stopped a few motorcycles."

"You did what?"

"I stopped a motorcycle that was headed in my direction and then hopped on, and then another towards the airport, and then the last one towards here."

I was surprised and asked him to show me how he would stop a motorcycle to give him a ride.

Waving his right hand by his waist as if he were petting a large dog, he said, "You wave your hand to signal that you want the motorcycle driver to slow down. Then he stops and you ask him to drop you a few kilometers, because he's headed that way anyway. But you have to know when to get off. That's the hard part."

"So you hitchhiked on three different motorcycles?"

"Yes, I guess that's what you call it."

"Is it common?"

"Yes, a lot of people do it. It's the only way around in the city. The company doesn't give us transportation."

I expected him to be a little unhappy or disappointed, so I said, "Too bad."

Without a hint of sarcasm or disappointment, and with a genuine smile, he said, "Not a problem, sir. No issue."

We got into the rental car with the local driver and headed to Tushar's sales territory. It was supposed to take about an hour and half, so I started asking Tushar about how he works, what products he promotes, how his customers perceive his job, and about the day-to-day challenges of being a sales rep in one of the toughest territories in the world.

Tushar had been with his company for seventeen years and was at ease with himself and his surroundings. He had neither the overenthusiasm of a young, ambitious man just out of college nor the stale persona of someone who's been there and done that. His job was to provide doctors with medical and scientific information about his company's products, which the doctors would then use when recommending a medication to their patients.

Tushar's main product was also sold by about a dozen or so competitors, who offered exactly the same product under different brand names. But there was one small difference between his company's product and those of his competitors: his product was slightly more expensive. Tough job, especially in India, where most people live on less than a dollar a day.

On our way, I asked how he saw the evolution of the sales force these days. How had things changed, given the growth of the Indian economy? What were the age groups of the sales force? Were they older or younger? How much did they make these days? How was morale? How had changes in technology changed the sales job in India? As a former salesperson, I am always curious about the changing nature and evolution of the field.

"It hasn't changed much since the last time, probably," he answered. "We have a lot more younger generation coming in, but they never seem to stick around in one job for too long."

"What do you mean?"

"Well, they typically enter the sales profession with another company, work for three or four years maximum, then hop over to our company to get the brand on their résumé. Often they are getting paid the same as those of us who have been here longer . . . and are loyal."

I thought this might be a sore point, so I suggested we change the topic.

"I don't mind talking about it anymore. It used to bother me a great deal at first, and sometimes it still does. That someone else is making more money simply because they came from another company. Or if they're in a higher position because of some internal political reasons. I don't think about it."

Then we arrived at one of the largest hospitals Tushar was going to take me to, JJ Hospital. It's a government hospital, and I felt familiar nausea as we walked in and saw crowds of people everywhere. White bandages covering an eye; blood-stained shirts that seemed to have dried over a day or so; the smell of ammonia diluted with brown water. It seemed that good old-fashioned government hospitals hadn't changed since I'd last been in one in the late 1970s, when I lived in India.

One of Tushar's colleagues, who covered that territory and that specific hospital account, met us in the lobby to take us upstairs to meet one of the most important customers, a cardiologist. It was only 11:30 a.m. and already about ninety degrees. There was a throng of people waiting for an elevator that probably hadn't been serviced since the 1950s, and I began to get a little nervous about being in such a hot, tight space with sick patients.

One of the patients standing in front of us began coughing—one of those deep coughs that take about a minute to finish.

I am so outta here. I am not about to get in that rusty sardine can with him.

I suggested that taking the stairs might be good, for some exercise.

As we arrived on the sixth floor, huffing a little, I saw sick patients all over the floor of the long hallway—some recovering, some just admitted, some eating with their families along the corridor, with nothing but thin, whitish sheets to separate them from the coldness of the floor. They were just lying there. No beds. No room.

Walking through the maze of sick patients, Tushar encouraged me to keep walking, assuring me that this was normal.

When we arrived at the cardiac catheterization lab, we were told that the doctor was not available.

"The doctor asked us to meet him here at this time," Tushar pleaded with the head nurse, who directed us to the small waiting area that served as a doctors' lounge. It was about eight feet by eight feet and had two small sofas with torn cushions that seemed to be burned around the side. As we waited, and waited, and waited, we realized that the doctor we were waiting to see was doing an emergency procedure.

After an hour and half, we finally got to see the doctor, who walked up to us with his surgeon's gear still on and put out his hand to say hello. We started talking while his nurse took off his gear, and then he sat to chat. He had a calm demeanor and seemed to be on friendly terms with Tushar. I realized that, because I was a visitor from headquarters, Tushar had taken me to some of his friendlier customers, but he still had a clear grasp of the product and a terrific, genuine relationship with the doctor.

After a few minutes, the nurse ran in and told the doctor he was needed in the operating room. That was our cue. We said thank you and took our leave.

Apparently feeling a little guilty that we had spent two hours waiting for a two-minute sales call, Tushar said, "Monday mornings are tough."

"I've been there, Tushar. No need to explain. Don't worry. I understand completely."

As we headed into Mumbai traffic toward the next hospital, I asked Tushar about his life, whether he had a family, how old he was, and how long he'd been a rep. He told me his son was in a local college and his wife was at home. He didn't make a lot of money, by any means, but he seemed content.

"The twentieth of the month is always the hardest," he said. That was the day the bills were due. "But we make it work somehow. No issue."

For the next few hours, we visited a handful of other customers spread throughout a more modern building, about an hour away from JJ Hospital. This hospital was a little cleaner because it was private and served Mumbai's middle class. Nonetheless, it was very crowded, not only with patients but also with lots of sales reps from competing companies.

The waiting area for our next doctor was packed with patients. We took a seat, waiting for the nurse or receptionist to call our name.

"Mondays are tough," Tushar repeated, and I was getting the feeling that my request to spend a day in the field with a Mumbai sales rep had made his life a little difficult that day.

While we waited, I tried to make him a little more comfortable by asking him more about his family and what he did on the weekends. Like most sales reps in India, Tushar worked six days a week, Sunday being his only day off. Most weeknights, he was in the field meeting his customers until about 10 p.m.

"They are more relaxed from 7 p.m. to 10 p.m., after they've finished seeing their patients," he said. "I feel great when I get to talk with them so openly around that time. We're all a little more relaxed then."

On his day off, for the previous several years, Tushar, his wife, and a handful of neighbors had gone door to door around their neighborhood, asking people to donate old newspapers and magazines, which they sold by the pound to a wholesaler. Then they took the money to a secondhand medical supplier and bought old medical devices—crutches, wheelchairs retrofitted for India's dirt roads, neck braces, arm devices, and so on. And one Sunday every month they went to a village about four or five hours from Mumbai and held a health fair, donating these supplies to handicapped kids living in rural poverty.

As Tushar was telling me this story of his life outside of work, I was in awe, thinking what a wonderful thing this was to do. I also noticed a great enthusiasm on his face that I hadn't seen all day. I started to get choked up as he showed me the photos of handicapped kids in the charity's home-made brochure, which he carried with him in his backpack. It breaks your heart.

Just then, a competitor's sales rep arrived. He was younger man with serious intentions of impressing the manager he was traveling with that day by getting past all the patients in the waiting room. I had to shake myself out of thinking about those little kids when the door opened and the doctor was about to call in his next patient.

Tushar somehow managed to get in front of the line of seven people and throw in his "Hello, sir" with a smile. The doctor saw him and told his staff to ask the patient to wait for a few minutes while he met with Tushar and me.

The sales call with the doctor went very well. Tushar initiated a brief but substantive conversation about some information that the doctor had not seen on previous visits, and after a few minutes we were done. We thanked the doctor for his valuable time and headed back to the waiting room.

As we stepped outside the door, about a dozen people rose, all thinking they would be next. Among the growing crowd there seemed to be more competitor sales reps, waiting for their chance.

"Do you know any of the competitor reps?" I asked. "Or how they're promoting their products? Or how they're positioning *your* product?"

"Not really," he answered.

I was surprised at his response, so I inquired further.

"Don't you want to be prepared and understand how to promote against them?"

"Why bother about them when I can do nothing about them and they change so frequently?" he answered, almost philosophically.

There was something about Tushar that intrigued me. During the two-hour car ride back to the hotel, he seemed as relaxed and comfortable as he had been in the morning. I asked how he dealt with all those competitors.

"I mean, how do you sell against sales reps who are promoting the exact same product, only a different brand? The competition is overwhelming. You don't have the basic transportation required to get around. You have to step over sick and bleeding patients to walk into the clinic to see your customers for perhaps one to two minutes. You have to fight with seven other sales reps just to be seen. It's a madhouse. It's a really difficult job. You've got so many people doing exactly what you do. How do you continue to move forward? It's amazing that you are able to be as successful as you are!"

Looking out the window as we drove by skyscrapers worth billions of U.S. dollars yet overlooking one of the poorest slums in all of Asia, he explained, "I don't worry about them because that serves no purpose. Rather, it is better to fix yourself and your mind than to try to understand other people. You can get lost in trying to think about what others say, think, or do."

He started to paint the colors around his story and it began to become clearer. A few years before, Tushar had been a very anxious and stressed-out person. He was a type A personality who used to plan, prepare, and execute. He was highly trained, motivated, and intent on high performance. He did what he was told to do—precall analysis, postcall analysis, paperwork, expense reports, sales reports, and the rest. But the stress was hurting him.

He was overloaded by more information, more competitors to track, more complexity in trying to figure out his customers, increasing unpredictability in a growing but fragile economy, and he became overwhelmed, angry, and frustrated. He didn't know what to do because there was so much coming at him so fast.

Then the monsoon came. It was a year of severe flooding like no other year in the streets of Mumbai. On his way home to his humble apartment he saw many people made homeless by the monsoon, and he made up his mind to do something to help them. Tushar and his wife took all the food out of their meager cupboard and put it into a bag. Then they carried it to the nearest makeshift tent where some of the homeless were living and gave it all away.

That night, he told me, he carried home a joy he hadn't felt in years. He suggested to his wife that they ought to do more of that, because it was so important to help others, and she mentioned a guru from her home city of Chennai who spoke fervently about giving to others as a way of gaining salvation for the soul. Skeptical but a little curious, Tushar went to see the guru speak. He was sold.

And so began Tushar's transformation from what he described as a stressed person, overthinking about others, to a more serene man who now knew where to focus.

"I started to realize that what I was trying to do was to force things around me to change. Very easily, I would get so upset at what other people would say or do. But my guru taught me to mind my *own* business. To let things be as they are and not worry about what others do but to mind what I do. To concentrate all my efforts on improving myself."

Excited about sharing an open secret, he explained further.

"Before, when a street beggar would ask me for money, I would say no because I knew that he might not use that money for food but instead waste it on alcohol or drugs. But my guru said, 'That's not your concern. You take the action that you take without minding what the beggar does. Don't have opinions of others. Don't let the opinions of others affect you. Just let all opinions be still. Let the thoughts and actions of others be still.'

"I became happier the moment I stopped putting my attention on others. Now I don't worry about trying to understand others or try to change others. What I work on changing is me."

As we finished our trip together that evening, my body was exhausted but my soul was refreshed. I had learned a valuable lesson that day, not only about how a sales rep in Mumbai promotes his products with very little sophisticated technology, amid the logistical nightmare of getting around, with cutthroat competition and a complex environment, but also about how our own thoughts can prevent us from moving forward in life and succeeding in chaos. In the process of reordering his own thinking, Tushar also had realized that he was better off directing his thoughts at himself and focusing his actions toward serving others rather than spending energy on all the distractions of life.

CHAPTER 9

LEARNING TO CATCH THE BUS

Waiting for perfection will get you nowhere.

There are many times in our lives when we suffer from the waiting problem. We wait for the perfect moment, the right time. We wait until there's enough in the bank. We wait until the kids get older. We wait until retirement. We wait for the right circumstance, the right person, the right thing to say, the right job, or the right situation. We wait until things are the way we expect them to be, until things fit into our narrative of perfection. We wait for the time when we have full control.

But that time never comes, and we waste all those moments.

Waiting for perfection gets us nowhere, and it only breeds more worry, anxiety, and stress, because we are waiting for something that does not exist. There is no perfect job, no perfect partner, no perfect career, and no perfect moment. There are only people, jobs, and moments. And if we try to force our "ideal" situation on life, we'll be waiting, stressed and worried, for a long time.

I found myself engaging in this kind of thinking one day as I attempted to do what Indian locals do—catch a bus.

o   o   o

"I'm not sure that's a good idea," my cousin Vivek said, when I asked him to show me what it's like to take the public bus system around New Delhi. I was excited to be in India for a visit with my family and I wanted to reimmerse myself in the chaos-filled culture I was increasingly learning to enjoy. I wanted to learn all aspects of daily living. Rather than just being a tourist, I wanted to experience life as anyone else in India would. After all, I worked in the toughest city in the world, New York, and I could take anything—or so I thought.

With a serious look, such as a father might give to a child who wanted to drive the car, my cousin responded, "Maybe next time."

I insisted, persisted, and pleaded with him to take me on the bus that he takes to work every day. He finally relented.

We walked through the construction site of an adjacent building, on a back road for about a quarter mile, and then stood patiently at the bus stop with twenty or so other people, waiting for one of the famous Delhi Transport Corporation buses to arrive.

About fifteen minutes later, Vivek said, "OK, start running."

Puzzled, I looked at him and asked why.

"The bus is coming," he said.

So?

"Come on. Start running," he insisted.

Turning my head, I noticed the bus approaching, kicking up dirt in its wake. It was completely full, stuffed with people like a tin of sardines, overflowing even, with people hanging on to the sides, their curled fingers clutching the steel window frames. The area by the door held another handful of young men, who were standing one on top of another.

Self-doubt began percolating in my head, a voice saying, "You are not getting on that bus! It is too full. It's too dangerous. You'll fall off and hurt yourself. Seriously, you didn't come here to get killed. You're not from around here, Bob. You're soft. What do you know about catching this crazy bus? This is not your cup of tea. You're slow. You're not one of them anymore. This is so uncivilized. You've lost your groove. You know what? You're beyond this bus thing. You get the idea. Why bother? Just call a cab."

I couldn't really see the driver's face through the dirty windshield, but I suspected he had no intention of actually stopping. Instead, he slowed down a bit on his approach to our stop—and then he started picking up speed! All twenty or so people waiting, including the heavier folks, had started running. They ran, reached out, and grabbed on tight to one of the many windows or pieces of metal—anywhere on the bus that could hold them.

"You gotta be kidding me!" I said aloud, in spite of myself. I was paralyzed by this freak show. I froze. I wondered if this was a joke. It wasn't rush hour. Where were all these people going?

"It's not safe," I said. "Someone is going to get hurt. There's absolutely no way I am getting on that bus."

Vivek stopped running when he realized that his New Yorker cousin wasn't going through with it.

"Can't we wait for the next one?" I asked innocently. "There's got to be another bus with some seats on it, right?

Surely, it's not this way every time? How are older people supposed to fit inside? Doesn't anyone get hurt trying to chase these buses? There has to be a bus that is not as full."

"All the buses will be this full."

Vivek suggested that we head back and look for a taxi. I insisted on waiting to see if the next bus wasn't so full. Smiling, he agreed.

The next one was just as full. It came and went, leaving me to inhale the cloud of dirt that it left behind as a reminder of my inability to take action.

I was a little scared of getting hurt, but after I started to get angry with myself for not being able to muster up the courage to grab on, I became determined. Suddenly, I had one clear, singular goal in mind: to get on that bus.

"Enough is enough," I said to myself as the third bus approached. "I'm done waiting."

I broke free from that nagging voice of self-doubt the moment I put one foot forward to start the run. It really didn't matter if the bus was full or not; I was determined to get on it.

Once again, lots of people crowded the spot where the door was supposed to be. I ran for it and found a spot on the pole where I could get a sturdy hold. I almost slipped, but then I felt a couple of hands reaching to help me. I set my footing and got a position on the pole full of hands.

Just as I was about to smile and celebrate my success, I noticed the man standing next to me in the doorway. He released one of his hands to reach out and help a guy running behind get on the bus. After that man was securely on, he in turn reached out and helped someone else get on.

Firmly gripping the pole on that overcrowded bus, I realized I had silenced the voice of self-doubt in my head. It was such an incredibly uplifting feeling. I wanted more.

My cousin had also gotten on the bus, after making sure I got on securely. Smiling at me and giving a thumbs-up, he went into the sardine can and signaled me to do the same. I managed to squeeze my way through and we stood somewhere in the middle, standing shoulder to shoulder with countless others. I was smiling quietly, celebrating the tiny success of jumping aboard.

The real beauty of that bus ride was a joy that I was headed somewhere . . . anywhere. I was not waiting anymore and thinking about taking action; I had actually taken action.

I also was liberated from thoughts about the way things ought to be and had embraced things as they were. There is real joy and freedom in seeing something coming and, no matter how imperfect it seems, reaching out to take action, and in having some assurance that, once we do start running and grab on tight, helping hands will often help those who help themselves.

CHAPTER 10

SHE'S WAITING FOR ME TOMORROW

Serving a purpose or a person helps to
pull you forward.

The challenges are overwhelming. Sometimes we are a blink away from hopelessness, feeling as though there are so many problems all around—very few of which we can actually do anything about—that we simply stand there, not knowing how to get through it all.

But deep inside all of us lies a clue that can help us move forward through the chaos. It is a deep desire to be relevant, to be significant to someone or something greater than ourselves. With so much noise in our jobs and our daily lives, so much uncertainty in the world, we can lose sight of something that gives us joy and happiness and that propels us forward: the ability to do something that has real meaning for someone else.

o   o   o

I raided the minibar in my hotel room and loaded my hand-
bag with a bag of potato chips, a can of roasted nuts, a Coke,
Purell, a hand towel, and Advil, preparing to go to the village
later that morning. I had been to Indian villages before, but
for some reason I was anxious and a bit nervous as I thought
about all the things that could go wrong on this trip. Hope
the car doesn't break down in the middle of our trip. Hope I
get back before sunset. What if I can't get a cell signal?

As my car pulled into the village, about four hours from
any major city, I noticed a lot of buffalo walking around, but
no Prakash. He was supposed to be here by now. I reminded
myself to be patient, because in India things always go late
and something always goes wrong.

As I waited for Prakash to show up, my mind started to
go into overdrive and I began wondering why I had put myself in this position in the first place. I didn't have to make
this visit. It was nice to do, but why had I put myself through
such a hassle, driving all this way to a remote village just to
see how social workers help deliver health care to villagers.
I had seen the PowerPoint presentation. I got the idea. So
what was the point?

I had to be crazy.

I thought back to a phone call with my friend Dr. Thakor
Patel.

"Bob, you have to see for yourself all the good the
SEVAKs do. You can only understand so much from behind
a computer. These guys do such good work amidst some
awful conditions, and that's the only way to see how small
changes can make a big difference when it comes to improving conditions in India."

I had been considering doing some volunteer work in India and I had asked Dr. Patel about his charitable program. Dr. Patel is a retired U.S. naval officer who lives in Maryland. He still sees some patients at the Bethesda naval hospital, but he spends most of his retired life volunteering to improve health care in rural areas of India. About four years before, thanks to donations from friends and the generosity of a corporate donor, Dr. Patel had created a new charitable organization to help villagers in remote villages in the state of Gujarat get access to basic health care and sanitation.

He modeled this concept after what he had learned in the U.S. Navy, while working on a vessel that helped with disaster relief efforts around the world. He set up a core group of twenty-eight regular villagers who would serve as social/ health workers for their neighbors. They were trained to check blood pressure, to screen for diabetes, and to provide education about proper sanitation and ventilation in huts and homes. They would provide support in areas without doctors, nurses, or trained medical professionals.

Thanks to the help of a local friend in Ahmedabad, Gujarat, they now have four regional coordinators who lead a group of about seven local SEVAKs. The Hindi word *seva* means "to serve" or "in service of others," and the idea was to create a corps of local villagers who would serve in twenty-eight villages.

I was remembering all this when a tall, thin man with glasses approached my car with a smile. Prakash was in his midthirties. He was wearing a white long sleeve shirt, blue jeans, and sneakers that looked as though they had seen their fair share of travel in these villages.

"Hello. You must be Prakash," I said.

"Yes, sir."

"Thank you for allowing me the opportunity to be with you today, Prakash. I really want to understand what you do and how you do it."

"Yes, sir. Shall we go visit the first home?" he asked, diving right in.

As we walked half a block with the buffalo to a woman's house on a muddy dirt road, Prakash began narrating her story, referencing notes he had made from previous visits.

"Her seven-year-old daughter was brought to me because she couldn't get out of bed in the morning."

The mother saw us coming and knew we were there to see her daughter. Covering her head with her saffron-colored sari, she quickly went inside and returned with her daughter in her arms. She placed the girl on a makeshift rope cot of the type commonly found throughout rural India—not too different from the cot I had been born on some forty-two years before. Crying and covering her eyes, the daughter looked as though she might be paraplegic.

"She had trouble standing, sitting up, or doing anything at all," Prakash said. "I took her to the doctor, about fifty miles from here, at the government hospital, but the doctor said that he couldn't do anything about the bones that are sticking out of her back. She's disabled and cannot get up even to go to the bathroom."

Seeing the tears starting to form in the mother's eyes hit me hard. I started to ask questions about what the doctor's official diagnosis was, what treatment options were available, whether it was a money issue, a transportation problem, or something else. Prakash answered as well as he could, and with each response I felt more and more helpless. I felt sad and wanted to move on, knowing that it was not likely to get any easier.

Prakash told me about the next villager we were going to meet.

"This woman's husband is a farmer and has severe diabetes," he said. "They had never heard of diabetes before we came to their house. He refuses to take the medicine we have gotten for him."

The farmer was lying on his bed, unable to move, likely because he was drunk.

The next person we met was a woman in her sixties who had started getting headaches and had sought help from Prakash. He discovered that she had severe high blood pressure and had taken her to the government hospital to see a doctor. Since then, she had been taking her blood pressure medication and was doing well.

We went from hut to hut, home to home, house to house. We saw a ten-year-old boy with cerebral palsy, a fifty-nine-year-old man with high blood pressure, and a recently widowed woman who had gotten her first-ever toilet installed, thanks to Prakash. With each passing hour, I felt overwhelmed by the problems in just this one tiny village in India. I could only imagine how Prakash felt.

But he didn't look fazed by any of it. He seemed calm and purposefully sincere, focused on documenting the cases in his neatly organized folders and reading me the data points on blood pressure and so forth. As we started walking back to the car, he proudly listed some of the SEVAKs' successes in this village.

"When we first started, only five percent of the people in this village had a toilet facility. After helping them fill out the

forms the government requires, twenty percent of the villagers now have a toilet."

Nodding, I continued to walk toward the car, moving
faster as I observed the sunset. I didn't want to be driving
back from the village at night. Many accidents happen because of the narrow roads and the trucks that emerge at dusk.

Thanking some of the villagers who had gathered to see
us off, I asked Prakash how he was going to get home.

"No problem, sir."

I offered him a ride, and after much cajoling, he accepted.

I was emotionally drained and felt a wave of pessimism
come over me. I wondered how they were going to make it,
how they would survive. How did he do it? I had to ask.

"Prakash, I have to ask you: why do you do what you do?
You're not a doctor. You have no medical training. You can't
diagnose these people's problems. You can only check their
blood pressure, check their diabetes, and then take them to
a doctor far away, which they may not be able to afford.
Don't you get overwhelmed with all these problems of the
villagers?"

"Sir, you see, this woman I will be seeing tomorrow had
a blood pressure of 160 over 110 when I first met her. She
takes her medicine, but not regularly. I am supposed to see
her tomorrow."

Maybe something had gotten lost in translation, I
thought, because he hadn't answered my question. He was
giving a specific answer and probably didn't understand that
my question was on a higher level. Trying to better understand his purpose and motivation for this seemingly thank-
less job, I switched gears and asked him about his family,
how he found himself doing this work, and so on.

"I saw the advertisement for the SEVAK project in the newspaper and was searching for a job, so I called the number and was hired. I wasn't sure what it was, but it paid well and I could work within my own village and do other things, too."

Prakash gets paid about $100 per month, but the job is not secure. If the handful of U.S. donors stops supporting the project, his job will no longer exist. Even so, he seemed happy with this job, seemingly without stress or worry, despite the overwhelming odds he faced. Was this his purpose in life?

"So, why do you do it, Prakash?" I was trying to get to the heart of his motivation, to discover what made him get up in the morning. "Help me understand. You don't have a secure job. You're not a doctor. You cannot solve all these villagers' problems. You work in some of the worst conditions, with no toilets, no resources, and no way of knowing if you'll have a job next month. Why do you do it?"

"That woman with high blood pressure . . ."

Oh, no, I thought. Not again with trying to explain that she's better off now that her blood pressure is controlled.

But with slow and deep sincerity, looking directly into my eyes for the first time, Prakash said, "That woman with high blood pressure is waiting for me tomorrow. I must see how she's doing. She's waiting for me."

This time, finally, I understood. Prakash continues to serve, despite difficult circumstances, because he is compelled by a duty higher than himself. This duty doesn't push him ahead; it actually pulls him forward by the strings of his heart. He is able to get through the challenges he confronts each day because he hopes to affect just one human life. He has no grandiose visions of a greater purpose, doesn't know what the future will hold for him, but his daily actions are brought into focus by the belief that someone might benefit, ever so slightly, from his effort, his work, his life. He is compelled to rise each morning, despite tremendous problems, because someone needs him. That woman needs him. She is waiting for him.

CHAPTER 11

LEARNING TO EMBRACE THE CHAOS AT THE KITCHEN TABLE

You're not going to get there
in a straight line.

Sometimes we are held back from pursuing a path out of fear of taking a chance, or by the perceived risk of deviating from the status quo. But is the status quo really that static?

I recently learned a lesson, not in India but at my dad's kitchen table: the most fundamental principle governing our existence is that we are born by sheer luck, randomness, and chance. We didn't get here in a straight line and we're not going to move forward in a straight line.

We have been living in the fabric of chaos all our lives, without realizing it. Chaos determines our birth; our meeting of friends, partners, and colleagues; and some of life's greatest experiences. Why are we fighting it? Why are we stressing out trying to control something that has brought us into this world and has introduced us to the people we love?

o   o   o

After making a handful of trips to India over a number of years, I was thinking about how to move forward in my career. I thought of taking a chance at something new I was considering. The pros-and-cons debate went on in my head for what seemed like forever, and with each passing week I was getting increasingly anxious. I was weighing each aspect, each trait; I dissected every possibility, any potential consequence of a step forward.

Then the phone rang. My dad was on the line, asking me to pick up the kids from his house a little earlier than usual because he had a doctor's appointment. He wanted my help looking through myriad test results, MRI reports, drug benefit plans—the usual chaos of navigating health care for an aging parent for whom I was responsible. It had been a routine doctor's appointment but he wanted my perspective.

When I arrived, we sat together at the kitchen table going through all the papers from the various doctors' visits. I couldn't make sense of it—and I also just didn't want to. Bigger issues of my own were weighing heavily on my mind.

My dad noticed my lack of concentration and focus and asked, "What's going on?"

"Nothing, Pop. All good." I didn't want him to worry. I was supposed to be looking after him, not the other way around.

"How were your trips lately? Where did you go in India? How's the blog and writing coming along?"

"Oh, nowhere special. I'm writing about all our experiences in India over the years. That trip up the mountain to visit Vaishno Devi. I spent a day in the field with a sales rep in

Mumbai and went to see some crazy hospitals. Then I went to a village. That was kind of fun, but scary. And, well, actually I visited a guru in this village a few hours from Mumbai."

As I was telling him about my experiences, some of which he had experienced with me, he leaned back, smiled, and started to ask me questions as if he himself had been on a similar journey: "Is that place still there?" "Is that hole-in-the-wall restaurant still near the bus stop?" "Did the guru look at your hand or was he more of an adviser?"

"You've been to these places, Pop?" I asked innocently.

"Sure, some of them sound very familiar."

"How did you go to Mumbai?" I asked. I somehow thought he had never left the village where I was born.

"Sure I went there, and lots of other places, even though we eventually landed in Rampur, where you were born. But I started . . ."

As he began to explain his own life journey, I realized that I had never really asked him about his experiences. I kind of knew in general but I had never heard the tale in such vivid detail as he was telling me now. Or maybe I had never paid close enough attention. I guess I wasn't really ready to receive it in my younger years. Now, in my forties, I was a father myself and at a crossroads in my life.

My father's journey was in chaos from the beginning. He bounced around among distant family members in different villages and small towns throughout a handful of areas in India, searching for a job. Through economic turmoil, political strife, famine, health disasters, poverty, violent eruptions, and drought, my father moved around, kept trying and searching, finally landing a job as an accounting clerk at a bank. Through a completely random series of events, he found himself in a small job in a small town in the middle of nowhere.

In that small town, he met his future wife—my mom—by sheer chance. In those days, a boy met a girl through their parents or family members and the two were not allowed to date or speak to each other. A decision was made about the other person based on knowledge of the person's family.

I was intrigued to learn so much about my dad over the kitchen table, and I began to see him in a different light. Parts of his story were similar to a number of experiences on my own journey. This conversation was richer in detail because it was rich in resonance.

"What's the real problem, son?" he asked after finishing his story.

"I don't know, Pop. It's a crazy world out there these days. Hearing your story makes me realize that you didn't have it any easier back then. I mean, it seems like the 'good old days' weren't as good as I thought.

"My problem is that I am trying to figure out how to go ahead with a life and career decision. It feels like I'm taking a big chance and I'm not sure if I should do it or not. I'm trying to cover all the angles and figure out how things will turn out."

Without even asking me the topic of my great introspection, he smiled and said, "You know, every day I get up and give thanks for the chance I've been given in my life, where I came from and where we are now, having the Dairy Queen store where your mom and I love going to work every single day. We are really very lucky. What are you so afraid of? Look at how I happened to find myself, out of all places, in that town, where I met your mom and we got married.

"Don't you get it? You were born by chance. And you have been living in a world full of chance. Why are you so afraid of something that brought you into this world in the first place?"

CHAPTER 12

MEETING
THE GURU

You can answer all your own questions.

When we're stuck and don't know which direction to go in life, we often seek advice, refuge, and guidance from those around us, experts, sometimes even the stars. It can be difficult to find our path, especially during times of uncertainty and unpredictability, when things are constantly changing so fast.

On the last trip I took to India before publishing this book, I spent a short time with a spiritual guru. It was a chance meeting, and although I didn't receive what I was expecting, I learned something even more important: if we only stop and listen to our own inner voice, we can find all the answers we seek and move forward in the direction we really want to go in life.

o o o

On a flight to Mumbai one Friday afternoon, I happened upon a magazine article about a parrot that was trained to pick out a tarot card, foretelling a person's future.

"A parrot? Picking tarot cards? Seriously? You might as well throw a coin up in the air, for crying out loud," I thought, brushing aside any hope of finding answers to the deep questions I had about my own path in life.

I'm a bit of a cynic, a skeptic who has worked on the streets and in corporate offices in New York City. I'm not much of a believer in palm reading, forehead reading, thumbprint reading, or the ability of any other appendage to ominously foretell my fate.

But deep inside, completely outside of my normal intellectual and cynical demeanor, I had this crazy desire for someone to drag me to one of these places to get a reading done. Partly, I suppose, this was so I could make fun of it or criticize the so-called spiritual guru who would tell you to do the sorts of odd things I had heard about: wear yellow, don't eat certain foods on certain days, feed a street dog, or some oddity reserved for those thirsty for inspiration. I wasn't going to drink that Kool-Aid. I was normal, right?

Still, a part of me was desperately in search of answers to help me deal with the uncertainties of life, and something about my recent days of feeling heavy with questions about my future tempted me to find a way to see one of these guys. I don't believe anyone can tell me my future, but no answers were appearing in my own mind. So, in an act of desperation, I wanted to reach out and see what the stars could see that I could not.

India is full of life gurus, with great variations in creed, message, format, products, and so on. Some have their own TV shows, some have a small following in their village, and some rotate through different towns, offering guidance, doling out advice, teaching yoga, and healing the mind and body.

In Mumbai, I reached out to an old friend who had recently retired from my company's U.S. division. Makarand (or Mak as he likes to be called) had settled in the United States during the 1960s and had spent most of his adult life working for one of the largest companies in the country. Seeing the emergence of India, he had recently retired from the company and had become a consultant for Indian and U.S. companies wishing to do business together.

Mak's home is in Connecticut, but he had an apartment in his hometown of Pune, India, a rising second-tier metropolis a few hours from Mumbai. When I told him I was coming into Mumbai and would be free to have tea or lunch on Saturday, he said with great excitement, "Come on over, Bob!"

Secretly, I was hoping he had a few good contacts so that I could explore some new career opportunities, but my main purpose was to find a way to seek his advice. I was so exhausted from overthinking my career and my life that I was giving up, hoping he would tell me which path I should take forward in all the chaos at work. If I couldn't muster up the courage to see one of these gurus, Mak was the next best thing—and probably more relevant in my circumstance.

Reaching Pune was not easy. It was a three- or four-hour drive from Mumbai, although the new highway with a modern rest stop and a McDonald's made it much easier. And getting out of the airplanes, hotels, meetings, and conference rooms made me feel like an explorer, free to walk about and experience the fresh air of new things.

Soaking in the warm, sunny climate of Pune was delightful, as was the conversation with Mak and some of his local friends over coffee. Mak was still not used to Indian-style coffee and he constantly asked for the coffee to be a little stronger. "I need American coffee."

I was eager to get answers about dealing with the reorganizations, changes, and rumors at work. I started to ask him for career advice and inquired how he was doing during his golden years of retirement.

"I am loving my life! It's so much fun. I get to do what I want and can't wait to get up the next day to do work," Mak said enthusiastically.

I was surprised by such vigor and I jokingly said to the server, "I'll have what he's having."

One of Mak's local friends was a man my own age named Laxmikant. Sensing that I wasn't getting the answers I was seeking, Mak mentioned that I should try to see Laxmikant's father the next time I was in India. Inquiring further, I learned that Laxmikant's father is a revered figure and has a big following as a spiritual guru and adviser, not only locally but also in India at large, in Singapore, in the United States, and in several other parts of the world.

Providence? There are no coincidences. Was I being set up here? Whatever, man. I needed answers. I wasn't getting answers from anyone else, and this person's father happened to be one of those Indian spiritual advisers. Why not give it a shot? Maybe the stars will show me the way. . . . Or maybe he'll tell me something bad about my future and jinx me or something. Should I even be doing this? This is crazy. Calm down, Bob. Just go and give it a try.

"How can I see him? Does he live nearby? Will he see me today?" I asked, suddenly eager.

"He's about two and half hours from here. Let's see if we can do this," Laxmikant said, somewhat reluctantly. It was

Saturday evening and he didn't want to drive out there on a Sunday. In desperation, I gave him one of those "Please help me" looks.

On Sunday morning I got a phone call from Laxmikant saying that we would be leaving by 10 a.m. to travel to see his father. Laxmikant picked me up and we started driving toward the hills, leaving the noisy city behind. The drive was picturesque, featuring rolling hills and beautiful pastures. It didn't look anything like the honking and dirty India that I had seen too often while navigating the metro areas in a taxi. It reminded me of the countryside of a small European nation, with lots of cows. The bright, sunny day bathed the road in front of us as we talked about life in India, life in the United States, and our ideas about work and careers.

In the back of my mind, I was considering what questions to ask the guru. I mean, how could I bring up substantive, important questions without sounding like a loser who has no idea what to do in life? How could I stop overthinking and worrying about the future? How could I get unstuck?

As we got closer to our destination, my mind started conjuring up ideas of what this so-called spiritual guru was going to be like. Images from the magazine article filled my head. Was he going to read my palm, run numbers using my birth date, read tea leaves? Would he ask me for a "donation"? He's got to be asking me for money.

Oh, man, what have I gotten myself into? I hardly know this guy and I'm traveling with him in a car for two hours to meet his father in a village where there may not even be a cell signal. My wife has no idea where I am. How do I know if this is even safe?

I started to get a little nervous, doubting myself as we reached our destination. Somehow, though, the sunshine-filled fields of corn and flowers, the clean streets, the warm air, and the big, beautiful trees dispelled my negative thinking.

Laxmikant got out of the car and some of the villagers approached and started touching his feet. He received them humbly, with folded hands.

"Are you a big deal, Laxmikant?" I asked jokingly.

Smiling with great humility, he led me on a tour of the village that bore his last name and his father's and grand-father's legacy. It seemed that growing up in this tiny town had been a wonderful experience for him, and he proudly showed me the temple and ashram, introducing me to some of the hundred or so people who had come from all over India to meet his father.

He led me down clean alleys and streets to a temple with many entrances. Attached to the temple was a small, open-air corner building. As we entered the temple, I noticed its pristine condition. Polished stones covered the floor all around us, with statues of the Hindu gods centered toward the back. A beautiful sand mandala of Vishnu adorned the center, giving rich color to the floor.

After we paid our respects to the gods, one of the guru's devoted volunteers in spiritual training came and escorted us through a hallway in the back of the temple to the other building, where the guru meets his followers. We went inside barefoot. The small room we entered contained a couple of sofas for guests and a small chair in the middle for the guru.

A beaming man of about five foot four with a fun, enthusiastic smile came in, lighting up the room. What he lacked in height he made up in the sparkle of his eyes, which seemed to indicate that he had discovered a secret he was eager to reveal.

We sat down and Laxmikant introduced me to his father, who began speaking in perfect English polished by his years of practicing law in a neighboring state. He offered me Indian sweets and we started chatting.

I asked how he found himself to be a guru and learned that his father had been a fairly famous spiritual guru who had contemplated the nature of existence over decades and began writing and sharing his knowledge. After his father passed away, Laxmikant's father quit his lucrative law practice and moved back to follow in his own father's footsteps.

As we began to get deeper into conversation, our focus shifted to life and knowledge of the self. He talked in detail about the ego, objectivity, human nature, Freud, Stephen Covey, and positive thinking, referencing great literature and thoughtful writers from yesterday and today. Eventually, we came to the question of what had brought me to this place. My skepticism wore off and I felt comfortable, almost eager to ask him the questions about my own life.

But something wouldn't let me reveal my own insecurities in front of Laxmikant. So I pulled one of those "When you speak to someone . . . hmm . . . and they ask you, Which direction should I go in my . . . I mean in their life, what do you tell them? Especially nowadays, when there are so many choices and so much confusion. There is no certainty anywhere and it can be confusing for some."

I tried to ask about myself without seeming too obvious. My ego wasn't letting go.

"Yes, you are right. It is very difficult for a lot of people these days to find the right direction to go in their life. Too many choices. Even if you go to a temple, you see lots of gods here in India. Too many to choose from. Which god should you pray to? And when you start praying, you get distracted and find yourself thinking of another god or of something else."

Pausing to reflect, he asked, "But let me ask *you* something. When you pray to God and ask Him all these questions—What should I do with my life? How do I earn more money? Whom shall I marry? How do I get through these difficult times?—does He respond? Does He answer you?"

Is this a trick question? I wondered. I mean, I guess the answer is no, but does he want me to say something spiritual or does he mean it literally? Do all the voices in my head qualify as God's voice? Or does he mean do I learn anything? What's he asking me questions for, anyway? *He's* the guru! He should be telling me.

Oh, man. I'm losing it. I'm way overthinking his question.

"No," I said to him, as if I was playing a TV game show and this was my final answer. "God doesn't answer." This was too hard.

"Right. God doesn't answer your questions because He is allowing you the time to answer your own question. You see, most people expect the answer to their life questions to be somewhere outside of themselves. But the reality is that God is allowing them that silence, that time, so that they can answer the questions themselves. Because the answer to all of your questions, the answer to which path to take forward, is always inside of you. It is not with-out but with-in.

"That's the true nature of existence, of life, of how to live life. To see the divine nature of existence within and to let it out. Let it breathe as you exhale, as you start your journey.

During times of prayer, God is allowing you to have a conversation with yourself, to resolve your inner conflict.

"The answers to the questions you have in your life are not found outside of your own mind. Your search for those answers often is revealed in moments of prayer or contemplation—or, other times, through the persistent questioning from an old man like me."

Sensing that I still didn't have the answer to my question about how to choose a path, he touched my hand. Giggling slightly, he said, "You know, some people think that I am here to give them answers to the questions they have, but my role is to be the stubborn person by your side, to help you ask *yourself* the right question."

With that, I realized that our time was up. Laxmikant rose and we said good-bye to his father. Hundreds of seekers thirsty for his knowledge were waiting in the great hall nearby. I was given a handful of books written by the guru and the guru's father on topics as relevant today as they were in the 1960s: inner conflict, objective view of the self, stress management, and more.

While we waited for lunch to be prepared, I got to see the guru's collection of books and sacred texts in the huge library, which was open to all seekers who dropped by the village. In addition to the hundred or so sacred Hindu texts, which were about two hundred years old, were thousands of more modern books from such writers as Napoleon Hill, Abraham Maslow, Viktor Frankl, Stephen Covey, and Wayne Dyer, covering topics as diverse as economics, psychology, philosophy, motivation, innovation, and architecture. Dozens of current magazines from all over the world were on display, including *The Economist* and *Time*.

Following the library tour, I was treated to a traditional Hindu lunch in the personal eating area of the guru and his family. On a brightly polished floor beautifully decorated with a sand mandala sat a wooden platform surrounding the steel plate on which the food was served. Rays of sunshine broke through parts of the roof, illuminating the cleanliness of the floor. Eating with my hands, as is the tradition, brought back some memories of my childhood in India, and the authenticity of the moment reminded me that I was eating soul food.

On the drive back to the city, I was full of good food, but more importantly, full with a lesson that many seekers realize a little too late: in our search for fulfillment, happiness, and direction during times of great confusion, we don't need to look in some faraway place like a village in the hills of India. Rather, we should look in a place that is so near but so often overlooked: within.

THE BUTTERFLY EFFECT

The shocks of a life in chaos destroy any notion of the ordinary. Chaos tears down and strips away any notion of
human institutions of order, civility, expectation, structure,
or perfection, leaving us with the only truth—ourselves in
chaos, as life has always been.

At first we oppose it. Fight it. Complain about it. Reject
it like antibodies fighting an infection, offering up feeble at-
tempts to control. Exasperated, we cry, shiver, and fight until
we can't anymore. We find ourselves frustrated.

Then we let go, give in, and ultimately accept. We stop
overanalyzing, overthinking. We can't overthink when there's
nothing more to think about than the moment in front of
us. We finally stop asking why and turn our attention to the
now.

At last, we start trying. We start smiling, breathing, and
living. Touching, smelling, feeling, trying, working, serving.
We begin moving forward.

Relying on our long-suppressed instincts, our positive
nature deep inside, pulled forward by an unknown force,
we begin adapting and start realizing that this isn't so bad.
The obstacles we encounter become stepping-stones to great
things. Tiny steps become unanticipated leaps. Randomness

and chance become gifts that nourish us on our way forward. Time flies, and when we look back we realize that, although not everything in life goes as planned, it is a great ride and things do work out in the end.

Armed with nothing but our own minds, our two hands and two feet, we all have great power to make positive contributions to our lives, to the lives of those we love, to our workplace, and to the purpose we pursue.

When we see ourselves as more than human and feebly attempt to make predictions, to cast aspersions, to scheme and overplan, we get stuck, because chaos spares no one. We can begin to realize our fullest potential for a fulfilling and happy life by learning to let go of our ego's attempt at control, by accepting the unpredictable nature of life. We must stop overthinking, overanalyzing, and trying to predict, and simply move forward. Chaos never goes away. You learn to live with it, at times flourishing in it but mostly just learning to embrace the chaos.

When I first thought of the idea of *Embrace the Chaos*, I did a Google search on chaos theory and discovered something called the butterfly effect, the notion that a butterfly flapping its wings in Brazil can cause unpredictable, unanticipated consequences, such as a tornado in a faraway place like Texas. The butterfly effect posits that, in a complex, fast, interconnected system with lots of little actions performed by billions of actors, one tiny action can lead to a major, unpredictable shift.

I was led to write this book by a tiny flap of a butterfly wing, a tiny action that I took a few years ago when I said yes to a friend who asked me, "Hey, Bob, can you show me India?" As a result of that simple choice, my mind opened up. I got unstuck, feeling great about doing something fairly usual—accompanying a friend on a trip.

From there, I went in a lot of different directions. One thing led to another, and then to another, and soon I found myself in a place I never thought possible. In this new place I finally fit in, enjoyed what I was doing, and was surrounded by people I love and who support me. The tinge of anxiety surrounding my every word, posture, and thought was replaced by calmness, a smile, joy in every breath, and a step forward.

I believe that what life has in store for us is simply not predictable. After I learned to stop trying to predict and accepted the fluidity of life, I started living again. The stagnant air was released. In its place, I let in the fresh air of possibility, spontaneity, and surprise.

I'm hoping that this book will cause a butterfly effect in your life; that it will act as a catalyst for you to move forward and live a life that you want; that you will take the positive, sometimes painful, but necessary steps to transform yourself from a caterpillar to a butterfly.

It's your turn to say yes.

EMBRACE THE CHAOS
MANIFESTO

WE ARE LIVING IN CHAOS. LIFE IS UNCERTAIN, UNPREDICTABLE, COMPLICATED AND FAST. ACCEPT. IT IS WHAT IT IS. STOP OVERTHINKING, OVERPLANNING, OVERANALYZING AND TRYING TO PREDICT THE FUTURE. LET GO OF TRYING TO CONTROL THE CHAOS. JUST CONTROL YOURSELF, YOUR THOUGHTS, YOUR WORDS, AND YOUR ACTIONS. BE HERE. DO ANYTHING. SAY YES. SERVE A CAUSE, A PERSON OR A PURPOSE. TAKE A TRIP AND SEE THE WORLD. TAKE ACTION. YOUR SOUL KNOWS WHICH WAY TO GO. DIG DEEP. PUT YOUR MIND AND HANDS TO WORK. SMALL STEPS FORWARD CAN LEAD TO BIG, UNANTICIPATED LEAPS. GO WITH THE FLOW AND ENJOY THE RIDE. YOU ARE RESILIENT AND KNOW HOW TO IMPROVISE. GIVE RANDOMNESS AND LUCK A CHANCE TO SURPRISE. LET INTUITION AND SPONTANEITY BE YOUR GUIDE. STOP WORRYING. DON'T WAIT. THINGS HAVE A WAY OF WORKING OUT IN THE END. GO AHEAD . . .

Embrace the Chaos

Download the manifesto on: www.embracethechaos.com.

ACKNOWLEDGMENTS

I am deeply grateful and indebted to my wife, Shefali, for giving me the encouragement and strength to persevere through difficult times in life. Her positive attitude and thoughtful insights have been invaluable. Thank you for allowing me to work hard on this book, as I could not have done this without you. I am deeply grateful for your love and support.

To my two daughters, who looked me in the eye and said, "This is a great idea, Papa," and took my words and made them their own. To Mom and Pop, who have always supported me, not only with their words of wisdom but also with their perseverance and fortitude to work hard, do right by others, and simply believe. I draw strength from their example of leading a simple life and serving others in their own small way, running a Dairy Queen business in a small town. They get up every day to serve ice cream cones to make their customers happy. What a beautiful thing!

This book would not be possible without the generosity, positive advice, encouragement, guidance, and support of Joni Evans. I am eternally grateful for your friendship at a time when I needed it most. I am on this journey because of you, and I shall always be indebted to you for your calming kindness and warmth. You provided me with the inspiration I needed to explore not only writing about business but also writing about my own life. Thank you, Joni.

Thank you, Neal Maillet, my editor, who saw a spark in a story about a stressed-out guy in a taxicab in India. Through your keen insights, I got a chance to rediscover myself and my inner voice. This book is not mine; it is ours. Thank you also to Jeevan Sivasubramaniam, Steve Piersanti, and all my Berrett-Koehler colleagues for helping to bring this idea to life.

To my sisters, Shalu and Neelu: Your positive energy and enthusiasm for this idea has been remarkable and I value it greatly. Growing up serving cones at the Dairy Queen store with you both, I could never have imagined writing a book about life! Thank you Neer, Saurabh, Mehek, Arun, and Rita for supporting me through it all. I appreciate your patience and understanding.

I am grateful for my wonderful and talented literary agent, Laura Yorke, for encouraging me to start my blog on the weekends, for giving me the tools to make this work, and for believing in me. You are awesome!

To my friends—Bob Perkins, Suj Mehta, Craig Weinstein, Ritesh Veera, Jason Grossman, and many others: Thank you for being my audience and providing insights and great advice to help me write this book.

INDEX

ABOUT THE AUTHOR

At the age of nine, Bob Miglani moved to the United States from India with his family, who had nothing more than $75 and a desire to pursue the American dream. Growing up, he delivered newspapers, mowed lawns, and helped run the family Dairy Queen business, where he learned the value of hard work, doing the right thing, and serving customers with a smile.

Bob carried those values with him into his professional career in corporate America, where he has been working for twenty years as an accomplished executive with a Fortune 50 company in New York City. Whether as a top-performing sales rep or while creating new and innovative strategic functions for the company, Bob's work has taken him to more than thirty countries around the world.

Bob is the author of *Treat Your Customers: Thirty Lessons on Service and Sales that I Learned at My Family's Dairy Queen Store*, which is about doing the small things that make a big difference in creating a vibrant, customer-focused business.

Bob helped his wife, an optometrist, open her new practice in the midst of the world financial crisis in early 2009, while also trying to manage the chaos of life with two young children.

As an active speaker and a volunteer with the Albert Schweitzer Leadership for Life Program, hosted each year in Dublin, Ireland, Bob helps to motivate high school students and young adults to pursue innovative careers and life possibilities in a new, global world where anything is possible.

Bob is a board member of a prominent U.S.–India trade group and often provides advice and guidance to U.S. businesspeople who wish to do business in India. Bob is also an angel investor in a handful of technology startups in India, where he acts as a thought coach, mentor, and friend to the founders.

On occasion, Bob is known to take a handful of friends and like-minded souls searching for a fresh perspective on a fun and reflective personal seven-to ten-day life tour of India, inviting people to experience their own Embrace the Chaos journey.

For more inspiration, advice and self-assessment tools, Bob invites you to follow his personal blog, **embracethechaos .com**, where he discusses all that he is learning about life and work in chaos. He also invites you to join the conversation on his Facebook page **(facebook.com/bobmiglani)** or to reach out to him by e-mail, at **bob@embracethechaos.com.**

Berrett–Koehler
Publishers

Berrett-Koehler is an independent publisher dedicated to an ambitious mission: *Creating a World That Works for All*.

We believe that to truly create a better world, action is needed at all levels—individual, organizational, and societal. At the individual level, our publications help people align their lives with their values and with their aspirations for a better world. At the organizational level, our publications promote progressive leadership and management practices, socially responsible approaches to business, and humane and effective organizations. At the societal level, our publications advance social and economic justice, shared prosperity, sustainability, and new solutions to national and global issues.

A major theme of our publications is "Opening Up New Space." Berrett-Koehler titles challenge conventional thinking, introduce new ideas, and foster positive change. Their common quest is changing the underlying beliefs, mindsets, institutions, and structures that keep generating the same cycles of problems, no matter who our leaders are or what improvement programs we adopt.

We strive to practice what we preach—to operate our publishing company in line with the ideas in our books. At the core of our approach is stewardship, which we define as a deep sense of responsibility to administer the company for the benefit of all of our "stakeholder" groups: authors, customers, employees, investors, service providers, and the communities and environment around us.

We are grateful to the thousands of readers, authors, and other friends of the company who consider themselves to be part of the "BK Community." We hope that you, too, will join us in our mission.

A BK Life Book

This book is part of our BK Life series. BK Life books change people's lives. They help individuals improve their lives in ways that are beneficial for the families, organizations, communities, nations, and world in which they live and work. To find out more, visit **www.bk-life.com**.

Berrett–Koehler
Publishers

A community dedicated to creating
a world that works for all

Dear Reader,

Thank you for picking up this book and joining our worldwide community of Berrett-Koehler readers. We share ideas that bring positive change into people's lives, organizations, and society.

To welcome you, we'd like to offer you a free ebook. You can pick from among twelve of our bestselling books by entering the promotional code **BKP92E** here: http://www.bkconnection.com/welcome.

When you claim your free ebook, we'll also send you a copy of our e-newsletter, the *BK Communiqué*. Although you're free to unsubscribe, there are many benefits to sticking around. In every issue of our newsletter you'll find

- A free ebook
- Tips from famous authors
- Discounts on spotlight titles
- Hilarious insider publishing news
- A chance to win a prize for answering a riddle

Best of all, our readers tell us, "Your newsletter is the only one I actually read." So claim your gift today, and please stay in touch!

Sincerely,

Charlotte Ashlock
Steward of the BK Website

Questions? Comments? Contact me at bkcommunity@bkpub.com.

MIX
Paper from
responsible sources
FSC® C005010
FSC
www.fsc.org

Certified
B
Corporation
bcorporation.net